*Inside
American
Philanthropy*

Shall we devote the few precious days of our existence only to buying and selling, only to comparing sales with the sales of the same day the year before, only to shuffling our feet in the dance, only to matching little picture cards so as to group together three jacks or aces or kings, only to seek pleasures and fight taxes, and when the end comes to leave as little taxable an estate as possible as the final triumph and achievement of our lives? Surely there is something finer and better in life, something that dignifies it and stamps it with at least some little touch of the divine.

My friends, it is unselfish effort, helpfulness to others that ennobles life, not because of what it does for others but more what it does for ourselves. In this spirit we should give not grudgingly, not niggardly, but gladly, generously, eagerly, lovingly, joyfully, indeed with the supremest pleasure that life can furnish.

—Julius Rosenwald
1923

Inside American Philanthropy

The Dramas of Donorship

By Waldemar A. Nielsen

University of Oklahoma Press : Norman and London

By Waldemar A. Nielsen

African Battleline (New York, 1965)
Africa (New York, 1966)
The Great Powers and Africa (New York, 1969)
The Big Foundations (New York, 1972)
The Endangered Sector (New York, 1979)
The Golden Donors (New York, 1985, 1989)
Inside American Philanthropy: The Dramas of Donorship (Norman, 1996)

Library of Congress Cataloging-in-Publication Data

Nielsen, Waldemar A.
    Inside American philanthropy : the dramas of donorship / by Waldemar
A. Nielsen.
        p.   cm.
    Includes index.
    ISBN 0-8061-2802-X (alk. paper)
    1. Endowments—United States.   2. Philanthropists—United States.
I. Title.
HV97.A3N54   1996
361.7'4'0973—dc20   95-39302
                                                                      CIP

Text design by Cathy Carney Imboden. The text typeface is Minion.

The paper in this book meets the guidelines for permanence and durability of the
Committee on Production Guidelines for Book Longevity of the Council on
Library Resources, Inc.∞

1   2   3   4   5   6   7   8   9   10

—⁂—

Contents

Contents

Contents

—❧❧❧—

Illustrations

Following page 142

—✦❦✦—

Preface

This is a book of personal reflections and judgments about foundations and philanthropy in the United States. It is addressed primarily to philanthropists in the process of forming or revamping their foundations, but also to individuals working in philanthropy, and to people who simply have an interest in this special aspect of our pluralistic system.

In recent years I have had the unusual opportunity to get to know a considerable number of wealthy Americans in the throes of establishing foundations. Although I have been involved with foundations for a good many years, that experience has been a startling voyage of discovery.

In the prevailing view—or mythology—foundations are created through a process of cool calculation and rationality by purposeful, philanthropic donors. But what I have now come to understand is that in many instances they spring from the most personal and emotional factors imaginable: fear of death, hope for remembrance, tangled family relationships, power struggles, guilt, vanity, old resentments, and new illusions. They are sometimes the fruit of careful planning and premeditation. But in at least as many instances they are the product of negligence, impulse, idiosyncracy, or deathbed despair.

These vital and uniquely American social inventions of the American pluralistic system are as much creations of emotion as of premeditation. Which may explain why some have been unimaginably brilliant and others unimaginably disastrous—and many others somewhere in between.

This book is therefore an attempt to show the human dimension of foundations. The dramas of donorship chronicled in these pages challenge the prevailing pallid, reverential, legalistic, bureaucratic, intellectualized interpretations of philanthropic institutions, and take us closer to reality.

I would like to thank the Gannett, Commonwealth, Rockefeller Brothers, John D. Rockefeller 3rd, Leo Model, and Robert Wood Johnson foundations for their financial support of my work—and the Aspen Institute, which has been my institutional base.

I would also like to acknowledge my intellectual debt to those many dear friends here and abroad—including John Gardner, Margaret Mahoney, Elizabeth McCormack, Siobhan Oppenheimer Nicolau, Stephen Graubard, Asa Briggs in Britain, Julian Marias and Jose Antonio Munoz Rojas in Spain, and the late Paul Ylvisaker—who have all given me the great benefit of their counsel and ideas.

—Waldemar A. Nielsen

New York, New York

Part One

—⁂—

The Critical Factors

Chapter One

—ↄ᭡ᘓᨦᣘᢧ—

The American Context
and the Coming Wave

This is a book about modern philanthropic foundations, the unique role of the United States in spawning them, the imminent prospect of a vast intergenerational transfer of accumulated personal wealth in this country, and the implications of that historic conveyance for the American philanthropic tradition—and indeed for the future of the nation. It is also a book about their donors—the saints and scoundrels, the wise and the foolish—who have been the most influential component in shaping that tradition. They, and the foundations they create, may constitute a precious national resource for confronting the awesome challenges of the coming century.

Charitable institutions of many kinds, including schools, hospitals, orphanages, and monasteries, have of course existed for many centuries and in most parts of the world—sometimes as creations of princely authority but most often as religious institutions. Ancient Egypt, China, India, and Rome had them. Throughout history Judaism has honored the principle of individual charitable duty, and Jewish communities around the world today are notably philanthropic.

Christian communities, Protestant and Catholic, have developed along with their churches a vast apparatus of schools, hospitals, orphanages, and other charitable institutions that have flourished for many centuries. Moslems, as well, have a long philanthropic tradition. Today, for example, some twenty-five thousand private endowments, known as *waqfs*, exist in Teheran alone. And most Islamic countries have a special government ministry to oversee their operations.

Because of the universality and antiquity of such spiritual and charitable institutions, their great ruins can be seen from Tibet to Isfahan, from Saint Petersburg to Mount Athos, and from Jerusalem to Florence, Fontevrault, and Canterbury. These are moving reminders of the universality of the human impulse to altruism, as well as to the glory, vulnerability, and even corruption of many of the institutions created to administer it.

In the United States a special aspect of this great tradition of charitable initiative has been the development of the private secular philanthropic foundation. Linked neither to government nor to a religious body, these foundations have taken initiatives and performed tasks far beyond responding to manifest needs and directly alleviating human distress. They thus represent a special form of social entrepreneurship and a potential for creative responsiveness to opportunities for human service. They now exist in a number of western European and Latin American countries and in Japan, but they are still preponderantly an American phenomenon.

Private charitableness came to the United States with the first settlers and was sustained and reinforced by the immigrants who followed them. Philanthropy's structure and methods have changed in the generations since, but the force of the spirit underlying it remains undiminished.

After the American Revolution, small private philanthropic foundations began to be created for special purposes, ranging from the advancement of astronomical research to providing educational opportunities for blacks in the South to attacking the problems of slum housing in the cities of the North. Throughout the nineteenth century their growth in numbers and resources was steady but limited.

Then about a century ago, as a result of the formation of the first great private fortunes in this country, and perhaps because of the heroic spirit of that age, a new kind of philanthropic foundation was created that has become a distinctive American achievement: The inventors were a few men of the generation of John D. Rockefeller, who poured a large part of their wealth into these new institutions. Adding inspired leadership, they demonstrated the immense potential foundations have for improving the human condition. The impact of their creations was so dramatic that the face and force of philanthropy have never been the same since.

In the subsequent decades, as the whole continent was settled and as industries expanded and private fortunes were produced in every part of the country, foundations bloomed like flowers after the rain. New England and the mid-Atlantic states were the first to industrialize and spawn private wealth and foundations. Coal and steel and later automobiles brought wealth and foundations to the Middle West. Cotton and tobacco brought them to the Southeast, oil brought them to Texas and the Southwest, and agriculture, aircraft and electronics have now brought them to the West Coast.

Private foundations are now a distinctive national phenomenon, both numerous and rich. They are elitist institutions left remarkably free by a democratic, egalitarian society to involve themselves in almost any field—education, science, medicine, religion, the arts, and international affairs, among others. Not bound by voters, shareholders, or customers—and with only feather-light oversight by government—they couldn't possibly be allowed to exist with such potential power and such utter freedom of action in a democratic society. But they do.

Now, however, we may soon see a major, indeed momentous, growth in the number of foundations and in the scale of their resources. Thousands of individuals, with wealth ranging from a few million to several billions of dollars, will, with all the certainty of actuarial tables, die off in the coming two or three decades. Billions, perhaps trillions, of dollars of accumulated personal wealth will then pass into new hands, some to heirs and some to charitable trusts and foundations. A closer look at the magnitude of wealth that may be involved is necessary to give meaning to these anticipations.

The United States has just been through the most vigorous and sustained period of private wealth accumulation in its history. The 1980s, years of powerful economic growth and prosperity, enabled many baby boomers to become rich, and some very rich. *Forbes Magazine,* which tracks such matters, calculated that there are currently some sixty-four billionaires in the United States, and Kevin Phillips, a prominent political prognosticator, has estimated that about 210,000 Americans are at least "deca-millionaires."

The precise totals are not known, but one of the most carefully researched and highly respected of several scholarly estimates is that of Cornell University economist Robert Avery. Dr. Avery's estimates are based on the 1989 U.S. Government Survey of Consumer

Finances, which is designed specifically to collect wealth data. Given the fortunes currently accumulated, and assuming the growth continues, he calculates that intergenerational transfers of that wealth will total some $960 billion by the year 2000, $3.2 trillion by the year 2010, $6.5 trillion by 2020, $9.25 trillion by 2030, and $10.3 trillion by 2040. Put differently, Avery predicts an average of about $225 billion a year in inheritances over the coming forty years. These are the most astounding estimates of the accumulation of private wealth in the history of the country, and it is very possible that such monumental transfers, because of the special circumstances that made them possible, may never occur again.

As important as their sheer magnitude is the distribution of these anticipated sums. From the studies of Avery and others, it is known that among today's American elderly, wealth is more concentrated now than in any previous generation: about one-third of the total is held by the top 1 percent. Also, because wealthier people tend to have fewer children, a small number of individuals are going to get the bulk of the future inheritances: Best estimates are that 1 percent of the heirs will get a third of the wealth transferred, another 9 percent will receive the next third, and the remaining 90 percent will split the remaining third.

The implications of these transfers and the possible impact on American philanthropy come into focus when one recalls that there are now, after two hundred years of development, some 35,000 active American foundations with combined assets of some $175 billion—totals far beyond anything that exists in other nations of the world. But if only 2 percent of the estimated private wealth now accumulated is committed to philanthropy, as now seems quite possible, the number, assets, and grant making of American foundations will double by the end of the first decade of the new century.

If these numbers and estimates are realized, as students of the subject now expect, or even if they prove to be only approximately correct, the consequences for American society could be very great. This nation faces ominously deepening problems of health care, education, welfare, environmental degradation, drug addiction, crime, racial conflict, and other such matters that government and the political system have not been able to deal with effectively. Is it possible that the private nonprofit sector—with a massive new infusion of resources—could help significantly to get them under control?

It is therefore a propitious, indeed a crucial moment, to take a fresh look at this distinctive aspect of the American Way. Can this impending flood of philanthropic funds—free from the constraints of politics, pressure groups, or short-term congressional thinking, and benefiting from the ideas of the best of our scholars, scientists, and social reformers—make a significant difference in enabling American society to cope with, and ultimately conquer, some of its most threatening problems? There is no assurance that it can, but given the much feared immobilization of government our foundations are potentially a competent, non-self-interested, uniquely American resource to draw upon. In the past the best of foundations have given birth to important new institutions of higher education. They have built great new hospitals and museums and thousands of libraries. They have reformed American medical education, advanced whole areas of scientific research, given educational opportunity to many children of the poor and dispossessed, helped create our networks of public broadcasting, and helped provide better housing for many of the poor in our central cities.

Given the growing problems of American society and the anticipated cutbacks in government-funded social programs, foundations may be far more essential to the national welfare by the end of the century than ever before. It is also quite possible—according to economic and political analysts of the American future—that the influx of new resources that philanthropy is expected to receive in the coming two or three decades will be the last such gigantic infusion.

By this strange confluence of circumstances, it is possible that private philanthropy could become an instrument of salvation for an endangered democracy searching for answers to its most threatening problems. The likelihood of this outcome depends on the quality of performance of the next generation of foundations. How many of the thousands of new ones now in prospect will prove to be vigorous, relevant, and effective? How many will be mediocre and inconsequential? And how many incompetent, even corrupt? At their best, they could make a crucial difference, especially if governmental and political institutions have been stalemated.

The ability of foundations to make significant and timely responses to the growing social crisis in America will depend on two factors above all others—namely, the capability and commitment of their donors. Each of these individuals is at the start the standard setter of his or her foundation's relevance and effectiveness—and subsequently will be the driving force behind (or sometimes the drag factor on) the organization's performance.

It is to explore the basis for expectations in that regard—and possibly to help raise to some degree the effectiveness of the coming wave of new American philanthropic donors—that the following chapters are devoted.

Chapter Two

—⁕⁕⁕—

In the Beginning
Is the Donor

The first and fundamental fact about foundations is that they do not start with a concept or an organization chart or a strategic plan. A foundation starts with a person, the donor. That human being, by his or her major charitable act, is the fountainhead from which all else—good, bad, or indifferent—flows.

At the start the donor is all-controlling. From him or her come the money, the clear—or vague—definition of the foundation's goals (broad or narrow), the fields of its activity, the choice of its legal form (grant-making or operating), its life span (limited or unlimited), the choice of the trustees and the inclusion or exclusion of family members in its affairs, and the determination of its style (energetic or passive, creative or conventional) and its governing values (conservative or reformist).

Almost inevitably a foundation starts as a mirror of the donor's finest qualities or most glaring faults. In the great majority of cases the donor is the key factor in determining outcomes: good donors and good philanthropy go together, as do incompetent or indifferent donors and incompetent and indifferent foundations—and, in a few instances, corrupt donors and corrupt foundations.

Many foundations are set up in perpetuity, so a donor's faults can then be outlived and overcome, just as his or her courage and creativity can be dulled and lost over time. But until death intervenes, and quite often for a considerable period afterward, the donor's mark on a foundation is generally very strong. This is true even if he or she had no strong interest in philanthropy and no clear purpose or priority in mind when creating the foundation.

Donors on the whole are revered figures in the American context. Yet, oddly enough, they tend to become the forgotten factor in American philanthropy. Their fundamental role and special characteristics are often displaced by the changing outlooks of successive generations of their trustees, and even more by the preoccupations of staff professionals responsive to changing academic, intellectual, and social trends.

Still, donors are the human core and starting point of each institution. And, because of the vast wave of wealth transference now impending in America, understanding the phenomenon of donorship—its circumstances and complexities—is more important at present than ever before.

Who donors are is relatively clear. They are all, in greater or lesser degree, wealthy people. But they stand apart from the vast majority of other wealthy Americans in that, for one reason or another, they give or bequeath a significant portion of their wealth to philanthropy. The great majority of rich Americans do not.

Beyond that, donors differ in every possible respect—in age, in health and energy, in motivation, in family situation, in aptitude—or ineptitude—for philanthropy, in fields of interest, in social outlook, and in style of operation. They also differ in their state of mind and morale at the time of creating their foundations—ranging from hyperenthusiastic to deeply depressed.

Why donors become donors, their motivation in creating a foundation, varies widely and is interpreted very differently by different observers.

Some do it out of a spirit of simple altruism. Some do it essentially as an aspect of their "estate planning." Some do it out of religious belief. Some do it for publicity and to gain social status; some to try to perfume a sordid reputation. Some do it as a means of supporting a cause they believe in—education, the arts, health care, or whatever. Some do it out of affection for a community and locality. Some do it as a memorial to a mother, father, or beloved child. Some do it in the hope it will be a vehicle for "keeping the family together." Some do it with a clear purpose; but some apparently have nothing in mind except perhaps a hope of remembrance.

Philosophers and religious thinkers have always had difficulty explaining the altruistic impulse. It is subject to contrasting interpretations. Ancient religious texts and more recent philosophical and psychiatric theories have all cast much doubt on the inherent goodness of human nature. The Bible has man born in original sin and with a predisposition to selfishness. The portrait of human nature painted by philosopher Thomas Hobbes was one of the duplicitous and superficial character of human benevolence. Others, from Plato to Machiavelli to Karl Marx, have argued that humans are incapable of acting out of any other motive than their own self-interest. George Santayana, wrote that "In human nature generous impulses are occasional or reversible; they are spent in childhood, in dreams, and are often weak or soured in old age. They form amiable interludes, like tearful sentiments in a ruffian." In the same vein, John Steinbeck, author of *The Grapes of Wrath*, saw the "philanthropic streak in Americans as merely a euphemism for selfishness." "Perhaps the most over-rated virtue in our list of shoddy virtues," he once wrote, "is that of giving. . . . Nearly always giving is a selfish pleasure, and in many cases is a downright destructive and evil thing. One has only to remember some of the wolfish financiers who spend two-thirds of their lives clawing a fortune out of the guts of society and the latter third pushing it back. . . . Such a nature never has enough and natures do not change that readily."

Nevertheless, all the principal religions have honored altruism as one of the greatest of human virtues. And by the nineteenth century the word "altruism" had begun to make its appearance in the writings of social thinkers. Auguste Compte, Emile Durkheim, and Jean Piaget, among others, have asserted that it is inherent in human nature. Durkheim, who believed it exists in every society, wrote that it is not merely "a sort of agreeable ornament to social life," but its fundamental basis. Much earlier, Saint Paul, in his letter to the Corinthians, wrote, "And now abideth Faith, Hope and Charity, these three; but the greatest of these is Charity."

The twentieth century has provided both terrifying and inspiring evidence of both the pessimistic and the optimistic views of human nature. There was the horror of the Nazi death camps, for example; but there was also the heroic willingness of thousands in occupied Europe to shelter and rescue Jews even at the risk of their own lives with no thought of remuneration.

In the United States the history of private charitable giving constitutes another challenge to the skeptics. Only a small fraction of wealthy Americans—perhaps 2 percent—set up their own foundations. But this is a portion far larger than in any other nation. The resulting aggregate of some 40,000 functioning foundations operates alongside the far-more-massive charitable generosity of the great majority of individual Americans, poor and middle-class alike.

When donors set up their foundations, that is, at what stage in their lives they activate their giving, is a more fateful matter than is generally understood. The optimal moment might seem to be when an individual has had some substantial life experience but is still young enough to give his or her philanthropy some intelligently defined purpose as well as energy, leadership, and continuity.

There are such examples. Far more common, however, is the new donor who is along in years, whose energy is already in decline, and who is heavily preoccupied with matters other than philanthropy—including family and health problems. Such individuals may also be struggling with the painful process of retiring from their company—letting go of the position and authority that provided a status base for much of their life. Widowhood, illness, and inexperience in organizing a charitable institution may also be distractions and deterrents.

To be an aging or elderly apprentice in philanthropy presents heavy, even fearsome, intellectual, physical, and emotional demands. It is a simple enough matter to decide whether or not to make a gift to United Way, and if so how much to give; or even to decide whether one's alma mater needs a new dormitory. But if one seriously undertakes an effort to help cut the crime rate, raise educational achievement, improve health care, or improve protection of the environment, then the conceptual and the operational problems can be enormous. If a good many new donors, under such circumstances, turn out to be less than spectacularly effective, we should not be surprised.

A third even more difficult and almost equally frequent situation is that of the deathbed donor, the individual who may have had serious intentions to launch his or her foundation "at the right time" but who has been overtaken by a heart attack, stroke, or cancer before finally getting around to it. Suddenly, in these sad and desperate circumstances, a whole range of immensely important and agonizing decisions have to be made while Death stands waiting. Fears of dying, hopes of remembrance, regrets, physical pain, and emotional despair, or panic, can in such circumstances dominate the process of foundation creation—or not uncommonly turn it into an impasse of utter indecision—in effect the abandonment of the resources to others and to chance.

How donors go about setting up their foundations, given all the deep emotional aspects of the matter, is predictably mostly amateurish if not irrational. Since the great majority of donors in the past, most all of them men, have almost by definition been individuals with long experience in establishing major enterprises, it might logically be assumed that in launching what is often the last great enterprise of their life they would seek sound advice from individuals familiar with the field, review the experience of other institutions, assemble a board and staff of proven competence in philanthropy, and define the program of the new foundation on the basis of some study of social or scientific needs and opportunities.

But in most cases, if they turn to anyone other than a family member or old friend it is usually to their lawyer, accountant, or financial advisor. Tax, legal, and financial considerations take priority. Typically, donors make no study of the work of other successful and unsuccessful foundations. Quite often they will not define any clear philanthropic objectives of their own and will include in the foundation's charter simply the boilerplate language ordained by the tax code. They choose their trustees not for their competence in and commitment to philanthropy but for their familiarity. Thus the process is more often a deeply personal and emotional one than an exercise in rationality and objectivity.

Understanding the full human complexity of the process of donorship and foundation formation, including its emotional and irrational aspects, is essential to understanding the reality of American philanthropy, in all its diversity, its frequent failures, and ultimately its greatness. Getting rid of the overlay of sugary mythology about donorship and confronting the human challenge of it make the whole subject more comprehensible and far more fascinating. It makes understandable why nearly one-third of new large foundations—created by deathbed donors or indifferent donors without any real interest or experience in the nonprofit world—fall into serious and sometimes disastrous difficulties after their creation. It helps us understand why so many foundations, given money and little else by their founder, muddle along in mediocrity. And it helps explain why so many foundations fall under the control of staff professionals after the donor is gone: they were abandoned orphans from the start.

A full-length portrait of donorship and foundation formation also helps us understand the odd inconsistencies and contradictions: That some of the toughest old brutes in business were openly sentimental when it came to philanthropy; or that some donors who were the most cynical in money matters were remarkably naive in their charities, and that some who were broad-minded and forward-looking in the direction of their corporations were weak and indifferent in giving guidance to their foundations. Such a look also helps us understand something about the tradition of honor and civic responsibility in American life. Otherwise, how could the abandoned fortunes of unphilanthropic, corrupt, even psychopathic donors such as Henry Ford, Howard Hughes, and John MacArthur have been transformed after their death into useful, beneficial philanthropies by their trustees and staffs? Perhaps most important, a clear-eyed survey of foundation launching helps us appreciate the extraordinary achievements of those donors who managed to create great foundations—those rare individuals who gave their foundations not only funding but ideas, courage, and entrepreneurial skills.

In fact, the list of donors who have built the great American philanthropic tradition has included everything from the lowest criminal and psychopathic types, to benign nonentities, to heroes who have defied the conventions of their time to advance great principles, and organizational geniuses who effectively applied their creative skills from the world of business and finance to the totally different worlds of science, education, and the arts. So great is their range, and so unique, colorful, appalling, or inspiring are their stories, that the only way to convey adequately their distinct characteristics and their significance is to present a gallery of their full-length portraits. Broad overviews and summary statistics simply are not enough.

These adventurers, these planters of the money trees, these rascals, saints, and heroes, comprise a special breed of men and women. Their stories constitute the rich and real human saga of American philanthropy.

To convey a sense of the profoundly personal and emotional context in which many donors make their basic philanthropic decisions and commitments, the following are some actual quotations, some from biographical materials, and some from the author's experience in working with various donors over the years:

"He who dies rich dies disgraced."

"If I could, I'd just buy an extra big shroud and take it with me."

"I made the money. You guys'll have to figure out what to do with it."

"It's fun. It's exciting. It's like a kid in a candy store. I love it."

"I don't want to be forgotten. I don't want to be forgotten. That's what it's all about."

"I like to hear and touch the little ones we help. Their hugs and laughter are my reward."

"Setting up a foundation is like a premature death ritual. I can't face it."

"Frankly, my money is a lot bigger than my ideas."

"I'm doing this simply out of love for my dear dead mother."

"Getting is my forte. Giving it away just isn't my line of country."

"I believe God wants me to do this, and He will reward me."

"From this base, like that old Greek said, I could move the world. But where to? You got any ideas?"

"The supremest pleasure life can furnish."

"It all comes too late. Too late. And too many lawyers."

"My father died of cancer. My brother died of it. I have it. I want to help put a stop to this scourge."

"Getting even. Getting some respect. That's what charity gets you, and it's very sweet."

"This is going to be my mark, my little scratch on the face of eternity."

"I can do it. I can make a difference. I did it in my business, I can do it with my foundation. If God will just give me time."

"Giving little bits is easy. Giving big chunks is very hard."

"I love this town. That may sound dumb, but this has been my place on earth. So I have a debt to pay."

"Why, why, why didn't I start earlier."

"It's the rarest possible privilege a person could hope to have. It's being God in a small way."

Part Two

—⁓⁓⁓—

The Ultimate
Upside Potential

Chapter Three

—⁂—

Three Giants
of the Past

John D. Rockefeller,
Andrew Carnegie, and Julius Rosenwald

To put all that follows into perspective, let us begin at the summit, at the very highest point of American philanthropic achievement:

By a remarkable historical coincidence, three giants in philanthropy appeared on the American scene in the decades just before and after the turn of the twentieth century. They invented the modern philanthropic foundation and demonstrated its ultimate potentialities. And they marked the history of the United States indelibly by their works.

Their names were John D. Rockefeller, Andrew Carnegie, and Julius Rosenwald. All came from families of ordinary means, all gained great wealth as business entrepreneurs, and all devoted themselves and their wealth for a good part of their lives to philanthropy. Most important, all of them were able to apply to their philanthropy the same creative, entrepreneurial, and organizing talents that had brought them such extraordinary success in business.

Rockefeller, driven by his strong Baptist religious beliefs, saw himself as a servant of God and committed a large portion of his immense wealth to philanthropy. Carnegie, the immigrant son of impoverished Scottish radicals, was impelled by gratitude to his adopted country and a deep sense of social duty to help the poor and less fortunate to improve themselves and their condition. Rosenwald, son of immigrant Jews from Europe, was driven by gratitude for the freedom and equality offered by his new country and by a strong sense of obligation to all disadvantaged Americans and to Jews everywhere.

All three had immense scope and ambitions in their philanthropy—from nationwide reforms and institutional innovations at home to worldwide programs in medicine, education, and international affairs. They were truly giants in their vision, their skills, and their accomplishments. A hundred years later, the glow of their genius remains bright.

John D. Rockefeller Sr.

In the scale of his philanthropy and the magnitude of its impact on human well-being in the United States and around the world, John D. Rockefeller Sr. was probably the foremost of this formidable threesome. No donor before or since has equaled his achievements.

Paradoxically, in the first decade of the century Rockefeller was pilloried for his ruthless business practices. The press described him as "the supreme villain of the age" and "the most hated man in America"—judgments that later historians have softened considerably. Yet his generosity, practiced even in his early impoverished years, was never in question. The major organizations he brought into being include the Rockefeller Institute for Medical Research (now Rockefeller University), the General Education Board, the Rockefeller Sanitary Commission, the Rockefeller Foundation, and the Laura Spelman Rockefeller Memorial. His gifts to create these organizations totaled (at the market value of the securities at the time of gift) more than half a billion dollars, a sum that would be several times larger valued in current dollars. But the distinctive thing about the man's philanthropy was not its size but its quality—its great and pioneering objectives and its brilliant accomplishments. Almost everything since pales by comparison.

Rockefeller's philanthropy had its roots in his religious upbringing. He was a devout Baptist and saw himself as a steward of God. In his words: "I believe the power to make money is a gift from God. . . . Having been endowed with the gift I possess, I believe it is my duty to make money and still more money and to use it for the good of my fellow man according to the dictates of my conscience." Rockefeller's marriage fueled his social conscience. His wife Laura's parents, the Spelmans, were Congregationalists and ardent abolitionists. Her father was an operator in the underground railroad during the Civil War, and Spelman College in Atlanta (the first "advanced school" for black women in the South) was named for him and Laura's mother. Business, family, church, and charity were the circumference of Rockefeller's life.

In 1872, when his business was still small, Rockefeller gave some $7,000 a year to charity; by 1882 he was donating $25,000, and by 1892, $1.5 million. At that point Rockefeller's piecemeal giving, mainly related to his church interests (schools, hospitals, and missions), was putting staggering demands on his time and energy. After the announcement of one substantial gift he was inundated by some fifty thousand letters begging his help. Under great strain and in poor health, he was at the point of thinking he either "had to shift part of the burden or give up giving."

But then, by a fortunate confluence of circumstances, he made the most important single decision of his philanthropic career: he hired a young man of thirty-eight, Frederick T. Gates, to be his assistant. Gates at the time was the director of the American Baptist Education Society. He had just completed a study of the feeble state of Baptist colleges around the country, some of which Rockefeller had been helping with small gifts. Gates concluded that the need was for a great new standard-setting center of excellence in higher education, to be located not in the East but in the Midwest, which was then the rising new center of commerce and industry. Rockefeller was so impressed with Gates' report and by the man himself that he eventually gave a total of $40 million to bring into being the great new University of Chicago.

The process that led to that first series of exceptionally large gifts proved to be characteristic of Rockefeller's subsequent benefactions: hard businesslike evaluation of the concept, assurance of good organizational leadership, and unhurried pondering of the idea before taking action. His attraction to the large and exciting concept also was characteristic: he helped create the first distinguished university faculty west of the Atlantic seaboard (at the time the only two such American universities were Harvard and Johns Hopkins). The new super-university, dedicated to research as well as teaching, demonstrated Rockefeller's willingness to make a major financial commitment to a project he believed in.

Thereafter, as Rockefeller came to have increasing trust in Gates, the two of them became the most powerful and creative force American philanthropy has ever seen. They were such an odd couple that their relationship provides important insights into Rockefeller's particular qualities as a philanthropist.

Rockefeller was a reserved, taciturn man, almost stoic in his repression. He never raised his voice or showed emotion, and he always acted with great deliberation. Gates, in contrast, was passionate, eloquent, and daring in his thinking—part missionary, part entrepreneur. Sometimes overbearing but never less than forthright, Gates could thunder at Rockefeller, "Your fortune is rolling up, rolling up like an avalanche! You must keep up with it! You must distribute it faster than it grows! If you do not, it will crush you and your children and your children's children!" And Rockefeller, ever open to Gates' ideas, would listen.

These two men, joined by Rockefeller's son JDR Jr. after the turn of the century, made a team that has never been matched. Gates seems to have been the energizing and initiating factor, but the precise role played by each, and particularly by the senior Rockefeller, is difficult to judge because of the reticence of the man and his indirect style of leadership and control. Illustrative of this is the founding of the Rockefeller Institute for Medical Research. In 1897, after reading about the accomplishments of the Koch Institute in Berlin and the Pasteur Institute in Paris in finding cures for diseases such as anthrax, Gates proposed to Rockefeller that he create a similar American medical research institute. Rockefeller agreed. Then, in his usual fashion, he consulted leading medical figures in both the United States and Europe and steps were taken to ensure that the outstanding American medical scientists would join in the enterprise.

In 1901 Rockefeller was prepared to make his commitment, and the institute was established. It soon became one of the great centers of medical research in the world. Over the years it has produced a stream of Nobel laureates and major research discoveries.

In all, Rockefeller put more than $60 million into its work. In 1954, with the help of his grandsons, it was converted into Rockefeller University, still one of the world's leading centers for research and advanced training in the biological sciences.

Just two years after the launching of the medical institute, an even more ambitious enterprise was organized, the General Education Board. Gates and JDR Jr. played the leading roles in creating this new entity, whose accomplishments over the next twenty years, in bringing about changes in the post–Civil War South, were revolutionary. The board made effective use of liberal and persuasive southerners rather than outsiders to gain acceptance for its efforts to change the region's traditional approach to education. It infiltrated state educational offices with a small army of "missionary specialists" to promote the idea of publicly supported schools for whites and blacks. It made grants to improve the competence of primary school teachers and supervisors. And when it became clear that most of the benefits of these efforts were going to white children, not blacks, Rockefeller himself gave a polite but powerful prod to the board to correct the imbalance. Subsequently, the board offered to subsidize the appointment of special officers in state departments of education throughout the South who could devote full time to the improvement of black schools.

Later, recognizing that a more adequate tax base was needed to develop a system of public schools, the board began a broad attack on the problem of rural poverty. It introduced agricultural experimentation and farm demonstrations throughout the region, programs that were later taken over and supported by the federal government.

After 1912 the General Education Board undertook a sweeping program to overhaul and upgrade American medical education, which at that time was far inferior to the standards of European schools. The board based this effort on an explosive report prepared by Abraham Flexner with the help of a grant from Andrew Carnegie—a report that exposed the wretched inadequacy of American medical schools at the time. The board's medical education program, which ultimately cost tens of millions of dollars, stands as perhaps the single most dramatic achievement in the history of American philanthropy.

An offshoot of the General Education Board, the Rockefeller Sanitary Commission was set up in 1909 to eradicate the scourge of hookworm in the South. Dr. Wallace Buttrick, head of the board, had encountered in the course of his travels a public health official, Dr. C. W. Stiles, who was an authority on the disease. Stiles made a convincing case that it could be cured and prevented at low cost. Buttrick, persuaded, went to Gates, who took it to Rockefeller. After a year's careful study, the new commission was created with a major grant. Over the next five years the commission's attack on the disease reached hundreds of thousands of homes and millions of individuals. In 1915 the final and triumphant report on the project stated that the mission of curing and preventing hookworm throughout the South had been accomplished.

While this succession of large undertakings was underway, Gates began looking ahead to the creation of a massive new Rockefeller trust "to promote the well-being of humanity worldwide." In 1909, Rockefeller had indicated he was prepared to consider such an idea. His experience with the Institute for Medical Research and the General Education Board had convinced him that significant results could be achieved by placing large funds at the disposal of independent boards of expert and statesmanlike men. He had also come to know several administrators, including Buttrick and Dr. Wycliffe Rose, a former philosophy professor, in whom he had full confidence.

In his methodical and practical way Rockefeller had been mar-shalling the human resources needed for the last and climactic phase of his philanthropy. Thus he made the decision to create the first great global philanthropic foundation, for which he estab-lished a trust in 1909 with an initial conveyance of $50 million. Be-cause of Rockefeller's terrible public reputation at the time, it took three years of political wrangling before the Rockefeller Founda-tion was chartered. But as soon as that was done, the new institu-tion took off in a series of ambitious initiatives. Its International Health Commission, modeled on the old Sanitary Commission, began a global attack on hookworm and eventually on malaria, yellow fever, and other contagious diseases—with dramatic success. Its China Medical Board built the huge Peking Union Medical Col-lege, which became the center of modern Western medical knowl-edge in Asia.

The Rockefeller Foundation then launched efforts to build up permanent governmental machinery in the United States and abroad to deal with problems of public health. With the help of the foundation, the first major schools of public health and public health nursing were established here and abroad.

By the early 1920s this immense explosion of creativity had begun to subside. Gates had retired, and Rockefeller, by then in his eighties, had withdrawn to enjoy his family and golf and to tend to his investments. He died in 1937, at the age of 98.

That John D. Rockefeller Sr. was preeminently successful as America's great pioneer philanthropist there can be no question. But the methods that produced such results are still not well un-derstood. In business Rockefeller's formidable success was due in good part to his remarkable powers of organization. With single-mindedness, foresight, and ruthless determination he created a great integrated worldwide company in the previously chaotic oil industry. He also displayed a talent for recognizing and gathering around him able associates and for delegating to them broad responsibilities.

Those same qualities, apart from the ruthlessness, perhaps explain his remarkable achievements in philanthropy. He was a charitable man but not a sentimental one. In what might now seem like a very nineteenth-century view, he was not interested in merely distributing money "for human uplift," that is, for simple charitable alleviation of needs. He believed that work and productivity were the basic source of human well-being and that the task of philanthropy was to attack the root causes of distress, not merely to alleviate symptoms, and to nurture those qualities that enabled people to help themselves. Indeed he believed that the mere redistribution of the blessings of life could be catastrophic for civilization.

Personally Rockefeller was not an eloquent or ingratiating person. He had severe limitations of education and outlook. He was not well-read, not much interested in literature, science, or art, not expertly equipped to work with leaders in education and social welfare. And—cold, analytical and detached—he was not even a likeable personality.

He turned to philanthropy compulsively, as a commitment based on his fundamentalist religious beliefs. To his philanthropic causes he applied qualities that had brought him success in the business world: single-mindedness, a talent for selecting strong associates, and a readiness to entertain big, bold ideas and to make major financial commitments in behalf of them.

Perhaps above all, Rockefeller was a strategic or executive donor, not a hands-on or meddling type. He visited his Medical Institute only once in his life and then only briefly. After setting up the General Education Board, he did not meet with it for the next five years. After establishing the Rockefeller Foundation, he never attended a trustees' meeting. This detachment, this control from a distance, has led some observers to denigrate his role in philanthropy, seeing him as a passive factor and Gates and JDR Jr. as the real architects of the achievements. This is a curious judgment, for no one denies JDR Sr.'s central role in the company even after his serious illness in 1893 and his "retirement" two years later. Although he rarely visited the company's offices thereafter, he still exercised a strong hand in its affairs for the next twenty years.

In his philanthropy it was Rockefeller who chose Gates as his principal advisor and who trained his son as the third member of the threesome. In all his activities, business and philanthropic, he was attentive, methodical, and decisive. It was he who finally approved every major project, its funding, and the selection of the trustees and key individuals who ran it. He was the principal, and they were his agents; recognition for what was achieved should, in fairness, be distributed accordingly.

Andrew Carnegie

Andrew Carnegie, the most generous of this great threesome, was an extremist in every sense—extreme in work, extreme in abilities and self-confidence, extreme in ambitions, extreme in his boosterism for everything in which he was involved.

A son of impoverished Scottish immigrants, Carnegie went to work at the age of nine. By fifteen he was a skilled railroad telegrapher, and by twenty-five he was on his way to financial success with the help of friendly superiors who were impressed with his extraordinary energy and talents. After a rapid rise as a railroad executive, he became a wealthy entrepreneur and investor in oil, iron bridges, mining, and steel making, eventually creating and controlling his own huge, vertically integrated coal and steel complex. In 1901, at the age of sixty-six, he sold out to J. P. Morgan for $480 million dollars and dedicated the remainder of his life to his various philanthropies and causes.

In business and in other things, Carnegie was a mass of contradictions. Son of a radical Scottish reformer, he always claimed an affinity for ordinary working people and a sympathy for their needs. But in his business dealings he constantly lamented that wage rates were too high, and in the infamous strike at his Homestead plant he backed the bloody suppression of the strikers. He was a savage and relentless aggressor in business; but he was a mamma's boy at home and could not marry until his mother had died, at which time he was fifty-one years old. In the United States Carnegie was an indefatigable booster for the business and political Establishment, but in Britain he bought a chain of newspapers to try to abolish the monarchy and the House of Lords and disestablish the Church of England. A firm believer in the survival of the fittest, he felt the poor should not be pampered; yet he gave away more than 90 percent of his fortune for philanthropic purposes in the last twenty years of his life.

This bundle of contradictions who had almost no formal schooling became a self-educated man highly knowledgeable about not only business and politics but also music, world affairs, and what would now be called public relations. He was an effective public speaker and a prolific writer in setting forth his "Gospel of Wealth." Two of his magazine articles, on the responsibilities of the rich to give to charity, were immensely influential and in their time stirred much intellectual controversy.

The essence of his thesis was that it is the duty of the man of wealth to set an example of modest, unostentatious living, shunning display or extravagance; to provide moderately for the legitimate wants of those dependent upon him; and, after doing so, to consider all surplus revenues which come to him simply as trust funds . . . which he is strictly bound as a matter of duty to administer in the manner which, in his judgment, is best calculated to provide the most beneficial results for the community—the man of wealth thus becoming the mere trustee and agent for his Poorer brethren.

Two years after Carnegie sold his company he retired from business to devote himself full time to philanthropy. He already had done his apprenticeship as a donor. Twenty-five years before, he had given a swimming pool to his old hometown, Dunfermline, Scotland. When some relatives approached him to make a substantial gift to their church, he compromised by offering to provide it with an organ—since he felt organ music was about the only good thing about Sunday services. By this act he stumbled into one of his largest initial philanthropic enterprises. As soon as his gift of the organ became known, he was swamped with similar requests from other churches throughout the country and from abroad. Ultimately he gave organs to nearly eight thousand churches, half in the United States and the remainder in other English-speaking countries. For a man who was nonreligious and who prided himself as a pioneer in "scientific philanthropy" based on systematic and rational principles, this was a considerable aberration. But Carnegie was not a man to be deterred by his own inconsistency.

In 1881, when his wealth was becoming substantial, he offered Pittsburgh a free library building if the city would stock and maintain it. He later gave an additional large sum for eight branch libraries. He also made gifts for an art gallery, a museum, and a music hall, all of which eventually formed parts of the Carnegie Institute, which, with still more gifts, came to include a system of technical schools, a women's college, a library training school, and a natural-history museum. By the time this huge project was finished, Carnegie had given it some $28 million in grants. In 1954 the institute and its large and handsome complex of buildings was merged into the newly created Carnegie-Mellon University.

In some respects this early philanthropic venture typified Carnegie's philanthropic approach and priorities and his reasoning in setting the conditions for his gifts. Because of his own experience as a self-educated person, libraries seemed to him the perfect means to help people help themselves. The technical schools would help people to gain skills by which to support themselves and do useful work. Art and especially music, Carnegie felt, were potent means "for refined entertainment and instruction for the people."

In his speech on the night the Pittsburgh library was opened, Carnegie said that when "this library is supported by the community, as Pittsburgh has wisely committed to do, all taint of charity is dispelled. Every citizen of Pittsburgh, even the very humblest, now walks into this his own Library; for the poorest laborer contributes his mite indirectly to its support."

Carnegie did not ask the city to maintain the art gallery and museum, because these "are to be regarded as wise extravagances, for which public revenues should not be given."

In the period prior to the publication of his Gospel of Wealth, Carnegie also began to offer free library buildings to other communities if they would meet his conditions for continuing support. This was to become his largest single program of gifts and was to make his name as a philanthropist known worldwide. Over the next few decades he gave more than $60 million for the construction of nearly three thousand public libraries in the United States, the United Kingdom, and other English-speaking countries from Canada to Fiji. These many gifts were made out of his personal office with the help of a small staff.

It was two years after the publication of his famous essays on philanthropy that Carnegie sold his huge company to J. P. Morgan for $480 million. At that moment he was probably the richest man in the world. Immediately thereafter he began to follow his own gospel and give away the bulk of his great fortune. The decade from 1901 to 1911 was an explosion of one man's philanthropy the likes of which the world had never before seen.

In 1901 he set up the Carnegie Trust for the Universities of Scotland to strengthen their research and teaching and to provide student scholarships. To this he committed $10 million.

In 1902 he created the Carnegie Institution of Washington, D.C., to carry out a vast program of basic scientific research and experimentation in astronomy, geophysics, botany, nutrition, thermodynamics, and other fields. It represented a major breakthrough in the organization of interdisciplinary research in pure science and was developed by Carnegie with the help of advisory committees of distinguished scientists. In a series of gifts, he provided $22.3 million for its establishment.

In 1903 Carnegie set up the Dunfermline Trust to provide cultural and recreational facilities in the Scottish town where he was born, and he gave it nearly $4 million. He also gave $1.5 million to build a Palace of Peace in The Hague as a seat for the Permanent Arbitration Court that had just been established for the settlement of international disputes.

In 1904 he created the Carnegie Hero Fund to give recognition to civilians who risk their lives to save another, and to provide pensions for their widows and dependents. For this he gave more than $2 million.

In 1905, in a major initiative, he created the Carnegie Foundation for the Advancement of Teaching (CFAT) because, as he said, "the least rewarded of all the professions is that of the teacher in our higher educational institutions."

Initially, the CFAT provided free pensions, but in time that was seen as impractical, and a contributory plan was devised. Known as TIAA-CREF, this plan now covers not only college teachers but employees of all kinds of nonprofit organizations and has become the largest private sector retirement system in the world. A trailblazing institution, it has shaped the private pension movement since its earliest days.

The second purpose of the CFAT was to carry out studies of needs in American higher education. Among these was the famous Flexner report that led John D. Rockefeller Sr. to his revolutionary reform of American medical education.

All told, Carnegie provided the CFAT with some $30 million in gifts to do its work.

In 1906, in another example of his mixing of monumental initiatives with personal and idiosyncratic ones, Carnegie set up his Simplified Spelling Board to try to promote simpler and more rational spelling in the English language. He organized an aggressive campaign and promised to give it steady support if he were convinced it could succeed. But it did not.

Carnegie threw himself into his philanthropy with zest and enthusiasm after his retirement from business, but as the decade wore on, he became fatigued with it, and his attention and energies were directed increasingly to his other passion, the quest for world peace. Earlier, at the time of the Spanish-American War, he had been as jingoist as any, but he later swerved in the opposite direction, denouncing war in all its forms as barbaric, "the foulest blot on our civilization."

When opportunities arose to support some peaceful initiative, Carnegie was quick to respond. In 1907 a Central American peace conference was held in Washington, D.C. One outcome was the creation of a Central American Court of Justice to arbitrate disputes. Carnegie donated the money for its building. A year later he gave the funds to build the Pan American Union building in Washington, again as a gesture of support for an initiative of international cooperation.

In 1910 he took a larger step, creating the Carnegie Endowment for International Peace. Its tasks were to study the causes of war, to aid the development of international law, to educate the public about war and its prevention, and to promote the general acceptance of peaceful methods of settling disputes. Carnegie gave it an endowment of $10 million. In his usual fashion, he declared his full confidence in the eminent board of trustees chosen to head this endowment and left them "the widest discretion" in the measures and policies they might adopt, so long as "the one end they shall keep unceasingly in view until it is attained, is the speedy abolition of international war between so-called civilized nations."

A year after establishing the Endowment for International Peace (CEIP), Carnegie made his last major and most important philanthropic commitment. He created a general-purpose foundation called the Carnegie Corporation. It was to use its funds for whatever cause or agency the trustees and their successors in future generations judged the most significant "in promoting the increase and diffusion of knowledge and understanding amongst the people" (see chapter 18). At the same time Carnegie transferred to it an endowment of $125 million, thus fulfilling his commitment to dispose of all his surplus wealth during his lifetime. In toto, he had reserved for his family only some $15 million out of a fortune of nearly $500 million.

In addition to his philanthropic efforts, Carnegie fired off an unending stream of letters and articles to various world figures in the years leading up to World War I and used his extensive network of friends in high places to press the cause of pacifism. But to no avail. Even the board of the CEIP formally resolved in April 1917 that "the most effective means of promoting durable international peace is to prosecute the war against the Imperial German Government to final victory." It was some years before the endowment could resume its intended program. This turn of events in Carnegie's final years was deeply depressing to him. He did live to see the armistice signed, however, and so did not die in utter despair.

No more dynamic meteor has ever flashed across the philanthropic sky than this diminutive Scotsman. Quixotic, contradictory, evangelical, cunning, wildly optimistic, endlessly creative, frighteningly acquisitive in one phase of his life and astoundingly generous thereafter, Carnegie seemingly is a figure who could not possibly have existed. But he did.

Julius Rosenwald

In the triumvirate of the great historic donors, Julius Rosenwald occupies a special and honored place. He was the most committed to making American democracy work and to the struggle against racial and religious intolerance. Like Andrew Carnegie, and unlike the inarticulate John D. Rockefeller Sr., he wrote a number of important philosophical statements about philanthropy and the responsibilities of the philanthropist.

The son of poor Jewish immigrants from Germany, Rosenwald

grew up in Springfield, Illinois, where his parents had a clothing store. He finished two years of high school and then went to New York in 1879 to learn the clothing business in a relative's company. During the years of his apprenticeship in the city, he also became keenly aware of the plight of the flood of impoverished Jews who had fled to the United States to escape the bloody pogroms then taking place in Russia. Ultimately he returned to Illinois, where he opened a clothing business in Chicago. In 1895, with his family's help, he bought an interest in a struggling new mail-order catalog company, Sears, Roebuck and Co. Once Rosenwald took over management, the enterprise prospered prodigiously. Within fifteen years, in that period before a federal income tax, Rosenwald's fortune had reached some $200 million.

Despite his remarkable success, Rosenwald was always modest about it. He once told a reporter: "I believe that success is 95% luck and 5% ability. I never could understand the popular belief that because a man makes a lot of money he has a lot of brains. Some very rich men I know who have made their own fortunes have been among the stupidest men I have ever met in my life."

As his own wealth grew, Rosenwald began to play an active role in the affairs of Chicago. He took his civic obligations very seriously, and for the remaining decades of his life he was a force in most of the major efforts to improve life in the city, especially for poor immigrants and blacks.

From his days as an apprentice in New York, Rosenwald had always had a strong charitable bent. At that time he told a friend, "The aim of my life is to make $15,000 a year—$5000 for expenses, $5000 to be laid aside, and $5000 to go to charity." And, in his later years, the scale of his giving in fact followed the steeply rising curve of his wealth.

By 1912, when he was fifty years old, Rosenwald was giving away some $500,000 a year, not in accordance with a grand philanthropic plan but in the form of many small gifts to charitable organizations and needy individuals, each with his personal approval. In addition, he had begun a series of large matching gifts for the construction of YMCAs for blacks in more than twenty-five cities throughout the United States. He subsequently launched a similar program for the building of YWCAs for black women. This was in a period when there was a vast migration of blacks from rural southern communities to northern urban centers. The new facilities provided them not only with shelter and recreation but also vocational and other educational courses. These initiatives won Rosenwald nationwide attention at the time.

As Rosenwald's giving grew, so did the demands upon him. He was forced to hire an assistant to screen the hundreds of funding applications that flooded in from all over the country and from various other parts of the world. But he still made all the grant decisions. For him this was a joyous thing, not a chore, and it gave him great personal satisfaction.

From his experience with his style of hands-on giving, patterns evolved that eventually defined Rosenwald's philanthropic approach: In all he did, he was strongly inclined to sympathize with oppressed and disadvantaged people, perhaps, as he once said, "because I belong to a people who have known centuries of persecution." His giving was nonsectarian; he gave substantial amounts not only to Jewish causes but to others as well.

He felt a heavy obligation to help his home city, but his giving gradually became national and then international in scope. He generally tried to leverage other gifts by his challenge-grant contributions, and with a good bargaining sense, he imposed strict conditions on his larger gifts. He strongly favored practical projects that helped people improve their conditions of life.

He tried to focus his giving, but not too much, so that the unexpected opportunity would not be missed. He required careful investigation of applicant organizations before making a grant, but he was also prepared to bet heavily on individuals who impressed him with their ideas and commitment. He learned as he went, and along the way he was remarkably open to inspiration by the ideas of others.

Also, as his experience with giving grew, there gradually took shape in Rosenwald's mind a deep concern about the prevailing practice among donors of committing philanthropic funds in perpetuity, a concept on which he later launched a sustained and influential assault.

The net result was that Rosenwald's philanthropy was down-to-earth, flexible, compassionate, and people- rather than institution-centered. Its spirit was personal and hopeful. As he once put it in a speech to a Chicago group, "[I]t is unselfish effort, helpfulness to others that ennobles life, not because of what it does for others but more what it does for ourselves. In this spirit we should give not grudgingly, not niggardly, but gladly, generously, eagerly, lovingly."

Rosenwald's greatest single achievement in philanthropy started in 1910, triggered by some unusual coincidences. In that year he came across two books that affected him profoundly. One was a biography of William H. Baldwin, a Massachusetts industrialist and Unitarian reformer with a strong interest in promoting educational opportunity for blacks and poor whites in the post–Civil war South. The other was the autobiography of Booker T. Washington, who headed the small, underfunded Tuskegee Normal and Industrial Institute in Alabama. Washington was a dedicated advocate of practical training in industry and agriculture for blacks, convinced this would enable them to improve their impoverished lives and their communities. "The individual who can do something that the world wants done will, in the end, make his way regardless of his race," he wrote. This was an idea with which Rosenwald, from his Jewish experience, profoundly agreed.

In the preceding decades other northern philanthropists had addressed this same problem. Among them was John D. Rockefeller Sr., whose General Education Board was actively at work on it. Rosenwald enthusiastically added his funds and energies to the task. He made numerous trips to Tuskegee with his wife and usually brought along groups of other northern leaders to arouse their interest. He made substantial gifts to Tuskegee itself, and in 1912 he began to give Dr. Washington funds to be used on a matching basis to build new rural schoolhouses in the region. In each case the land for each school had to be deeded by the local authorities, the completed building had to become part of the public school system, and both whites and blacks in the local communities had to contribute funds or in-kind gifts to the projects. The goal was for the whole task of black education ultimately to be carried out with public funds and community involvement.

Many of the stories of the sacrifices made by the local people are very touching. One old ex-slave emptied out his life savings of thirty-five dollars in nickels, dimes, and pennies and gave it all so that his "children and grandchildren could have a chance," as he said.

By the time Washington died three years later, in 1915, some eighty new schools had been built with Rosenwald's help in Alabama, Tennessee, and Georgia. As a memorial to the great man, Rosenwald then offered to build three hundred more. And then more after that.

Ultimately Rosenwald contributed to the construction of 5,357 public schools, workshops, and teacher's homes in 883 counties of fifteen southern states, at a total cost of more than $28 million. He provided 15 percent of the funds and induced 64 percent to be provided from local tax funds and the remainder from individual blacks and whites. The impact of the program was so great that in the years following World War I it was said that about 60 percent of American blacks who had completed primary school had been educated in Rosenwald schools.

In sustaining the program, Rosenwald had to brave strong social prejudices in both the North and the South. He was subjected to constant and severe criticism that he was undermining the social order, but such pressures do not appear to have deterred him in the slightest, and among blacks he acquired almost mythic status. His picture, along with those of Abraham Lincoln and Booker T. Washington, came to adorn many schools, homes, and shacks throughout the South. Schoolteachers sometimes even built him into their arithmetic problems: "If Mr. Rosenwald had six dozen eggs, and if he bought four more eggs, how many eggs would Mr. Rosenwald have?"

In 1917, as the demands of the school building program grew, Rosenwald took the first step in forming an organization to distribute his many gifts. He set up the Julius Rosenwald Fund with a board made up entirely of family members, a small staff, and a branch office in Nashville to oversee the schools program. This proved to be only an interim step on the way to the creation ten years later of a fully organized and professional foundation

If one of Rosenwald's priorities in his philanthropy was to help American democracy work, the other was faithfulness to his duty to help Jews in need. The years during and following the First World

War were marked by a succession of grave crises for the Jews of Europe. In the war zones in Eastern Europe the suffering of the Jewish populations was especially severe; during the period of the Bolshevik Revolution in Russia, they were the target of a White Russian program of pillage and murder in which tens of thousands died; and in 1921 there was a devastating famine that further decimated their ranks.

In response, Rosenwald's philanthropy became international with a series of major donations for Jewish relief. But in the process he had to confront painfully difficult policy choices, and he became subject to severe criticism by elements of the Jewish community itself. This was the period following the Zionist decision to create a new homeland for the Jews, and each new wave of calamity produced passionate new drives for funds to resettle the victims in Palestine. But Rosenwald was firmly convinced that Jews had to find their salvation in the societies where they lived, not by being transported to a new "homeland." Moreover, he believed Palestine could never become economically viable and that massive funds from abroad would always have to be poured in for it to survive. The proper task for assistance therefore, in his view, was to help Jews obtain the skills necessary to gain dignity and acceptance in their own countries.

Because of these convictions, Rosenwald refused the importunings of the Zionists, and he put millions of dollars into such schemes as a huge project of the new Soviet government to resettle tens of thousands of Jews on large tracts of good farmland in the Crimea and the Ukraine. The Rosenwald money was used to help them become good farmers and to develop their new communities. The initial success of that program led him to give heavily to a subsequent plan to train Jewish workers living in cities in industrial skills.

Rosenwald's independent course brought him into continuous conflict with the Zionists and subjected him to severe pressures, especially with the subsequent reemergence of anti-Semitism in the Soviet Union. During the same period, however, he continued his work to improve race relations in the United States. He was relentless in his efforts to counter anti-black prejudice wherever it appeared—in education, employment, housing and military service. He was equally persistent in his efforts to counter anti-Semitism. An example was his long and eventually successful battle to force Henry Ford to stop his massive distributions of the notorious "Protocols of Zion."

In its earlier years the Rosenwald Fund had followed the lead of the Rockefeller philanthropies in working within the context of racial segregation to improve educational opportunities for blacks. Then, after World War I and the launching of the venturesome Laura Spelman Rockefeller Memorial, Rosenwald began to address basic issues of racial justice and the problem of segregation itself with grants to the pioneering Commission on Interracial Cooperation. In the late 1920s, as the commitment of the Rockefellers to this cause began to fade, the work of Rosenwald became even more impressive, supporting a number of organizations attempting to change racial patterns in the South. In addition the Julius Rosenwald Fund became active in the health field with grants for hospital development in the South and for the creation of experimental health centers staffed with black doctors and nurses in several cities in other parts of the country.

By 1927, probably influenced by his years of service as a trustee of the Rockefeller Foundation, Rosenwald came to believe that for a foundation to be a social agency rather than a personal convenience, it had to have a policy-setting body made up of persons of wide interests and experience, plus a strong professional staff. Accordingly, in the following year he replaced the family members on his fund's board. Consistent with his opposition to perpetuities, he specified that the foundation would have to spend all its resources within twenty-five years after his death. He also brought in as executive director Edwin Embree, whom he had come to know as a vice president of the Rockefeller Foundation, and who, like himself, had become discouraged by the growing conservatism of that organization.

The restructured Rosenwald Fund, while continuing its work to improve educational opportunities for blacks, then began a wide-ranging effort to find ways to lower the costs of medical care for the poor, both black and white, despite the strong opposition of medical organizations. He and Embree also launched a parallel program of conferences and studies on the general problem of black poverty and on such issues as the impact of farm tenancy and trade-union practices on the predicament of blacks in the South and in the North.

With the onset of the Great Depression, however, Rosenwald had to devote a large portion of his declining energies to the severe problems of his company. Even then he took the time, and a good part of his own fortune, to help shield hundreds of his employees from financial ruin because of the stock-market crash.

Rosenwald's final years were shadowed by two profound new developments: the rise of anti-Semitism in Europe and of Hitler in Germany gave new credibility and urgency to the idea of a Jewish homeland in Palestine; and in the United States, leaders in the push for racial equality began to be increasingly critical of what they regarded as his accommodation to educational segregation in the South, which his school-building programs had tacitly accepted.

Considerable disappointment must have accompanied his feelings of accomplishment from his philanthropy in that period.

Rosenwald died in 1932, just at the advent of the New Deal, but the activities of the Julius Rosenwald Fund continued. Under Embree's leadership the fund cooperated actively with various federal agencies, placing specialists within them to encourage attention to the special needs of urban and rural blacks. But some of its earlier initiatives in education and health care, which depended heavily on governmental services and outlays, had to be aborted because of the condition of the national economy.

Embree remained at his post until 1946, at which time, eleven years ahead of the deadline fixed by the donor, the fund closed its doors. Despite the profound changes taking place both domestically and internationally during those years, Rosenwald's foundation remained a shining beacon in a very dark time, and his record as a philanthropist was extraordinary to the very end. He was a great humanitarian and believer in democracy. His generosity was based on a solid and clear set of principles and convictions. At home and abroad he sought to be a social healer, a conciliator, a unifier. He had done his utmost with his money and his dedication to help alleviate the problems of disadvantaged people in his country and his world in his time.

Comparisons and Contrasts of the Old Greats

In their philanthropy as in their business life, all three of these giants were imbued with the spirit of a heroic period in American history when optimism and belief in the inevitability of progress was in the air. In the rough struggle for national development and industrialization, John D. Rockefeller Sr., Andrew Carnegie, and Julius Rosenwald were tough and victorious competitors.

But all three in their fashion were idealists with a firm faith in education, science, and the possibility of human brotherhood. Perhaps it was out of such convictions that their philanthropic efforts derived; certainly, crass considerations of tax advantage did not matter to them, since the first federal income tax was not enacted until after the bulk of their gifts had been made. Whatever their motivations, all three took their philanthropy very seriously throughout their lives. It was not a mere sideline or incidental interest; it was a major priority, and they worked hard at it.

These men began their giving early in their working lives, and their philanthropic involvements grew steadily as their wealth increased. Each thereby went through a long learning process, progressing from smaller gifts and simpler projects to larger and more complex ones. For all three the learning experience and the evolution of their philanthropic interests and ideas continued throughout their lives.

In style, the three differed greatly. Rosenwald was a hands-on giver with close personal involvement and control in his projects. Only in his later years d᾽ᴊ he delegate significant responsibility to a professional manager. Carnegie personally conceived and crafted his projects, not only their purposes but also their structure and manner of operation. But once they were established, he was ready to turn them over to boards of trustees (whom he personally selected). The boards had wide latitude in directing operations and, if necessary, even in redirecting them. Rockefeller relied heavily on his formidable assistant Gates and on his son to develop plans and programs, but he reserved for himself the final decisions on activation and funding. He was a power behind the scenes, but nonetheless very much a power.

All three men, from their business experiences, were skillful negotiators in arranging their gifts, and they were quick to perceive possibilities of using their gifts sometimes to leverage additional support from other sources. Carnegie and Rockefeller prudently spread their bets over a number of free-standing programs and institutions they created, even though each finally put the large remainder of his funds into a general-purpose foundation established in perpetuity. Rosenwald made substantial gifts to various projects and organizations, but he was not a spawner of new institutions, and his own Julius Rosenwald Fund, in accordance with his opposition to perpetuities, went out of existence fourteen years after his death.

Perhaps the most striking feature of their philanthropy, as we perceive it more than half a century later, is the heroic scale of the three men's ambitions and enterprises in contrast to the generally timid, piecemeal efforts of the great majority of large donors and large foundations today. For some reason these giants had a vision and boldness scaled to the vastness of their wealth. They also had the courage of their convictions in that they were prepared to make major, even huge, financial commitments to achieve the objectives they set. They also had the courage not to be deterred by controversy and public criticism of their efforts.

Finally, it is clear that both Rosenwald and Carnegie, despite certain disappointments in their last years, derived great excitement and satisfaction from their philanthropic endeavors—not merely from the public recognition and applause their efforts received, but also because their gifts gave a meaning to their lives that even their great achievements in business did not provide.

In the case of Rockefeller, who was such a shadowy and indirect presence, philanthropy seems to have been the fulfillment of a self-imposed duty to God, but the dedication and ability of his son in carrying on the work must have warmed even that cold heart.

Chapter Four

—⁓✤⁓—

Three Formidable Successors

*Mary Lasker,
Arnold Beckman, and Walter Annenberg*

In the decades since Rockefeller, Carnegie, and Rosenwald blazed across the sky, the American tradition of philanthropy has diversified, proliferated, and been vigorously sustained. And although no such surpassing figures have appeared in the following decades, a number of extraordinary successors have come on the national scene. Of these, three of the most outstanding are Mary Lasker, Arnold Beckman, and Walter Annenberg.

Mary Lasker: Genteel Dynamo

Mary Lasker, president and driving force of the Albert and Mary Lasker Foundation after the death of her husband in 1952, was one of the half-dozen greatest American philanthropists ever. Her foundation had only a modest endowment, but with the benefit of her remarkable skills and talents, it has had more impact on national health policy, caused more funds to flow into medical research, and ultimately probably saved more lives than any other in the United States.

Lasker was born in Wisconsin at the turn of the century. Her first career was as a successful art dealer and businesswoman. In 1940 she married her second husband, wealthy Albert Lasker of Chicago, who has been called the father of modern advertising. Both of them had a strong interest in medical research, and two years after their marriage he surprised the advertising world by turning his multimillion-dollar company, Lord and Thomas, over to his employees so that he and his wife could launch a joint campaign as health activists.

In that same year, 1942, they set up their Albert and Mary Lasker Foundation with an ambitious purpose: to raise public awareness of the major killing and crippling diseases and of the urgent need to conquer them—starting with cancer.

National concern with and study of these problems were at a low point in the 1940s. The Rockefeller Foundation had given up on cancer, saying that there were "no leads to follow." The American Cancer Society was not spending a penny of its modest funds for medical research. Public ignorance and fear of cancer was so great that it was not considered proper even to mention it by name in the mass media. And, as World War II was coming to a close, the federal government was about to shut down its major research arm, the Office of Scientific Research and Development (OSRD).

Undeterred, the Laskers launched their first attacks. Within two years they had organized a campaign to generate research funds for the sleepy American Cancer Society. The campaign raised $4 million, an astounding feat at that time. The effort included such innovations as articles in *Reader's Digest* and radio appearances by celebrities like Bob Hope, which helped demystify cancer and proved the possibility of garnering broad public support for a war on the disease.

Immediately thereafter the Laskers were able to overhaul the American Cancer Society itself by greatly strengthening and diversifying its board. Within a few years it became the nation's leading voluntary health agency, and it has since raised hundreds of millions of dollars in private donations for its work.

In that same period Mary wrote a now-famous letter to President Roosevelt asking him, in view of the imminent demise of the OSRD, what could be done to ensure continued support for medical research in peacetime. Consequently, FDR asked the head of the agency, Dr. Vannevar Bush, to study the issue. This led to a widely acclaimed report, *Science, the Endless Frontier,* that eloquently outlined the benefits of a long-term relationship between government and medical research. Within three years of the Laskers' initiative, the budget for the National Institutes of Health increased from $2 million to more than $30 million a year, and support for the National Cancer Institute rose from less than half a million to more than $14 million.

Encouraged by that success, the Laskers set their sights on an even larger target—to change the health policies as well as the budgetary priorities of the federal government. This ambitious aim grew out of a conviction that any real war on cancer, heart disease, stroke, mental illness, and the other major killing diseases could be mounted only on the basis of such fundamental changes.

Their evolving strategy was bold and broad in scope, and the Laskers realized that the eventual cost of carrying it out would be enormous. But they had absolute confidence in the possibilities of medical research to find cures for the dread diseases. They also recognized, and this was perhaps their crucial perception, that the general public had to become involved as well as the scientific community, and that political pressure, lobbying, and networking among influential citizens were all necessary if their war was to be won.

Their approach anticipated brilliantly the advent of the era of citizen activism, popular science, and the mass media in the formation of public policy and in the allocation of public resources. Obviously, their efforts drew heavily on Albert Lasker's promotional genius and advertising experience. But in its formulation and even more in its eventual execution, their campaign drew mostly on the determination and the personal persuasiveness of Mary Lasker.

A major element in their strategy has been the use of public awards to attract public attention and thereby to advance various substantive objectives. In 1946, in the first and most important initiative of this kind, an annual program of Lasker Awards in Medical Research was announced. In the years following it became second only to the Nobel Prizes in this field. Indeed, it became regarded as a reliable predictor of future Nobelists, since some forty-nine Lasker winners, after a lag of a few years, also achieved that honor.

For the basic objectives of the foundation, the awards became a major national media event, dramatizing important new discoveries in medicine, educating the public, stimulating the interest of the Congress, and attracting outstanding young scientific talent into the medical field. The program also served for many years to keep the foundation continuously in touch with the major developments in medical science and with outstanding scientists everywhere. At the same time, the sheer quality and prestige of the program gave powerful support to all the other activities of the foundation.

In 1949, because the national press was giving so little attention to medical research, the foundation established a second awards program for outstanding achievement in medical journalism. Within a few years this resulted in the appearance of regular columns on health and medical matters in more than forty of the nation's leading newspapers, generally raising public knowledge and interest.

Building on the media's growing appetite for health and medical information, and as another means of increasing the nation's awareness of health needs, the Laskers began to publish an annual health fact book. It summarized the incidence and costs of crippling and killing diseases, as well as the money major funding sources were spending on research. Until that was done, legislators, reporters, and even the medical profession itself had no comprehensive and up-to-date source of information about the areas of need.

In 1952, as this broad strategy was just beginning to have its impact, Mr. Lasker died, ironically, of cancer. Thereafter, Mrs. Lasker's younger sister, Alice Fordyce, became her active partner, bearing much of the responsibility of conducting the annual awards programs. Through her efforts they were maintained at the very highest level of prestige and integrity. Mary herself focused her efforts increasingly on personally influencing key decision makers in government.

For the next thirty-five years she spent a good portion of her days in Washington, D.C., in relentless and persuasive pursuit of her cause. In this role of "public interest lobbyist" or "benign plotter," as she has been variously called, Mary Lasker was acting on her lifelong conviction that events do not just happen and that new ideas are not born out of thin air. "Continents have been discovered," she is reported to have said, "laws passed, buildings built, and books written because the right two people met at the right time and the right place. It's a personal world."

To that personal world of Washington she brought a formidable array of assets. She was a handsome, intelligent, articulate, and engaging woman. She was wealthy and well-known, and she had a wide circle of friends prominent in business, the arts, and politics. With the help of those networks she had access to virtually everyone of importance, not excluding successive occupants of the White House, whether Democrat or Republican.

She combined zeal with great energy. She also had consummate skill in bringing together powerful individuals from Congress, the administration, and the media with leading scientists to discuss issues of health policy and medical research. Over time, the cumulative impact of these small, selective dialogues became very great.

In the early 1960s those efforts were reenforced by the creation of a Lasker Public Service Award to recognize "individuals who have encouraged Federal legislation and support of medical research, or who have helped to implement public health programs of major importance." Over the next twenty years many of the major government figures who played leading roles in the evolution of health policy were honored in this way, including such powerful members of Congress as Claude Pepper, Lister Hill, former Health, Education, and Welfare Secretary Elliot Richardson, and President Lyndon Johnson. Whether one attempts to measure the impact of the work of the Lasker Foundation in terms of new health legislation, or the volume of funds flowing into medical research, or in terms of growing public awareness of health matters, it has indubitably been immense.

It should also be noted that parallel to her concerns with health matters, Mary Lasker maintained a small and sustained assault on "urban ugliness," making many gifts for the planting of trees and flowers in cities here and abroad. One glorious spring, for example, she brightened the gray canyons of Park Avenue in New York by carpeting the mall running down its center with hundreds of thousands of tulips and daffodils, to the delight of matrons and cabdrivers alike.

Mary Lasker and Alice Fordyce both died in the early 1990s, bringing to an end the Lasker awards (to the dismay of many leaders in medicine) as well as their various other programs.

The tributes that Mary Lasker had received during her lifetime were many and glowing. The eminent medical scientist Dr. Sidney Farber wrote, "The health of the world owes more to her than to any one person." When she was given the Presidential Medal of Freedom in 1969, the citation began, "[H]umanist, philanthropist, activist—Mary Lasker has inspired understanding and productive legislation which has improved the lot of mankind." Hubert Humphrey, former vice president, has said, "Medicare and Medicaid would never have happened without the labors of this great woman." And, in the words of Dr. Michael De Bakey, the heart-surgery pioneer, who served selflessly for many years as chairman of the Lasker Medical Awards jury, "Mary Lasker was an institution unto herself. Asking what her importance has been is like asking what Harvard has meant to this country."

For all prospective donors, the meanings of the Lasker case are many. It demonstrated the immense potential of the private grant-making foundation in using a variety of measures to accomplish its ends. It proved that even with relatively limited resources a foundation can move mountains—but only if those resources are combined with considerable talents and energy on the part of the donors. As a donor Mary Lasker takes high rank among the great philanthropists the United States has produced.

Arnold Beckman, Scientist Donor

Another of the most effective and interesting of the second generation of large donors is Arnold O. Beckman of California.

Born in a small prairie town in Illinois in 1900, the son of a blacksmith, Beckman was an outstanding chemistry student at the University of Illinois. He went on to take a Ph.D. at the California Institute of Technology, and then joined its faculty. In the 1930s he invented a meter to measure the acidity of lemon juice, and with the profits from that success he created a company that later became one of the world's largest makers of scientific and medical instruments. Beckman has resisted making public information about his wealth or his philanthropy, but his fortune after all his benefactions is estimated still to be $500 million or more.

As a scientist and inventor Beckman has supported higher education and research for many years. But in the past twenty years he has made a series of substantial and impressive grants through the foundation that he and his wife created in 1977. Among them have been the following:

· $10 million to the City of Hope Hospital in Los Angeles for research in neuroscience and immunology

· $11 million to the University of California at Irvine for the Beckman Laser Institute and Medical Clinic

· $15 million to Stanford University for the Beckman Center for Molecular and Genetic Medicine

· $20 million to the National Academy of Sciences and the National Academy of Engineering to establish a western headquarters

· $40 million to the University of Illinois to create the Beckman Institute for Advanced Science and Technology for research on processes of the human brain and their applications for computers

· $50 million to Cal Tech to create the Beckman Institute for Interdisciplinary Research in Biology and Chemistry, plus $15 million for other research projects.

In the decade of the 1980s alone Beckman's gifts of this kind have totaled more than $170 million. Their impact has been even greater because they have often triggered major gifts from other sources. Indeed, becoming a recipient of Beckman's philanthropy is regarded as a certification of excellence in the world of science. As one leading researcher has said, "It is almost like winning a Nobel Prize. . . . It shows that you are in the highest and best company in science today."

As a great scientist himself, Beckman has been able to make highly discriminating choices without a large staff. Indeed, for many years his foundation consisted only of himself and his wife, Mabel. Since his wife's death, he has added one employee. He does, however, rely heavily on the counsel of a few old colleagues from Cal Tech in making his decisions.

Within the broad area of science, Beckman has defined clearly the particular aspects in which his gifts are concentrated, namely basic, long-range research of the kind neither government nor the general public would be inclined to support. He has also been strongly interested in encouraging interdisciplinary approaches in biochemistry and biomedicine. Once he has selected a project and grantee, he has been prepared to commit substantial funds, and in a number of cases he has designed the grants to require the grantee to raise matching funds. Wherever possible, he attempts to leverage his grants in this way.

Now in his nineties, Beckman has faced the deaths of his wife and many close colleagues, and he is in the process of completing the distribution of his fortune. Speaking of himself and his wife, he says they "had planned to run out of money and breath at the same time," but he is now left with some hundreds of millions of wealth still to distribute.

Beckman is leery of the conventional model of a freestanding, perpetual foundation—he believes it could result in a needless bureaucracy. He also worries that foundation trustees and staff members "have not always proved faithful to the donor's wishes." Given this anxiety, and because his sole interest and motivation is the advancement of scientific knowledge, he intends to put the funds into a new kind of foundation attached to a university—"to take advantage of an existing bureaucracy and joining forces," in his words. The university would operate the foundation, he says, in the way the National Institutes of Health support health research: scholars from many disciplines would compete via peer review for grants. The university would manage the investments and handle the bookkeeping, receiving in return a portion of the annual income.

But Beckman has not yet fixed on a final plan. And he is even considering the possibility of shifting his research focus to a different field. "Times change," he says, so "maybe now we should go back and see what we can do about preparing little kids who are two, three, four years old to take a major part in life."

However he decides to distribute the remainder of his wealth, Beckman insists that it will not be in a spirit of generosity. "I'm selfish as can be," he says. "I hate giving money away." But he has brought to that "distasteful" task a dedication to scientific research, a creativity of spirit, and a quality of intelligence that ranks him with the best philanthropists in American history.

Walter Annenberg: Media Maecenas

To understand Walter Annenberg, a media tycoon who has been a massively generous donor for many years, one must begin with the story of his father, Moses Annenberg, who came to the United States from Latvia as a small child. Raised in poverty in a tough Chicago neighborhood, he was street-smart and ambitious while still in knee pants. By the time he was in his teens, he was well into the bare-knuckle business of selling newspapers; in fact, he had already become circulation chief of the Hearst morning newspaper in the city, the *Chicago American.*

That was only the beginning. Thirty-five years later Moses Annenberg owned a publishing empire that included the *Philadelphia Inquirer, Daily Racing Form,* and periodicals ranging from *True Detective* to movie fan magazines. But the centerpiece of his holdings was the daily racing wire, referred to as "the Trust" by the underworld and used by thousands of illegal bookies across the country to receive instantaneous racing results. By that time Moe Annenberg, as he was known, could boast the highest income of any American, some $6 million a year.

Federal authorities were convinced Annenberg was a racketeer and closely tied to the underworld. Unable to pin specific criminal charges on him, they resorted to the Internal Revenue Service and charges of tax fraud to convict him—as they had done with Al Capone a decade earlier. They also threatened to charge his only son, Walter, with violations.

After negotiations, Moe pleaded guilty so that the case against Walter would be dismissed. In 1941 the father began serving a three-year sentence. On his way to jail he told Walter it was time for him to get serious about business and that he would now have to run the family empire of more than eighty corporations.

Walter was then thirty-three years old, and up to that time he had shown little aptitude for the role suddenly thrust upon him. After dropping out of college after his first year, his life had consisted of little more than fast cars, late parties, and Hollywood star-lets. To make matters worse, many of the family businesses were in trouble. The IRS was in process of imposing an unprecedented $8 million fine on them, and Moe's estate was declared insolvent.

Walter was passionately convinced that his father was a great man who had been singled out unfairly by the government. He was determined first to get him released from jail and then to set the record straight. He visited him faithfully every week, and he mounted a frenzied letter-writing campaign to people of influence, pleading for his father's release. But to no avail. Moe died in July 1942, eleven days after being paroled due to illness. On his deathbed he said to his son, "My suffering has all been for the purpose of making a man out of you!"

Under the lash of that admonition, Walter within two years was able to begin the restoration of his father's crumbling empire. He broke its ties with any business that would give a hint of scandal. He strengthened management, consolidated various operations, and began to restore the conglomerate's profitability. Then, in a series of entrepreneurial strokes, he laid the basis for its immense growth in the future. He launched *Seventeen,* the first fashion magazine for teenagers, which became a brilliant success. Four years later, by sending a two-cent postcard to the Federal Communications Commission, he won the right to create the thirteenth television station in the nation, WPVI, in Philadelphia. And in 1953, against the advice of all publishing experts, he bought out various local television-listing magazines and combined them to form the monumentally successful national *TV Guide.*

By the mid-sixties Annenberg's company, Triangle Publications, owned two major newspapers, a string of profitable magazines, *Daily Racing Form,* sixteen television stations, and three cable companies. Cantankerous and brilliant, stubborn and farsighted, brutal and incredibly generous, this complex personality had become one of the most powerful and wealthy men in the nation. But Walter Annenberg had still not achieved the central mission of his life—cleansing his father's reputation and establishing his family's respectability. In Philadelphia, which had become his home base, he was continuously subjected to the most virulent kinds of anti-Semitism and social discrimination; even his aged mother, tagged as the "widow of a convicted felon," was a pariah.

The depth of Walter's sense of obligation to his father has been shown in various revealing and symbolic ways. The portrait of himself that he had placed in his headquarters office had the shadowy image of his father in the background. From the time he took charge, he had plaques displayed in his various places of business bearing words taken from a prayer for the dying, "Cause my works on earth to reflect honor on my father's memory." For a long time he also had his father's MLA monogram printed on the covers of his various publications, a sign of his respect and affection repeated millions of times.

Politically, Walter Annenberg has been an arch conservative and a longtime backer of Richard Nixon. In 1968, as a reward for his loyal financial and editorial backing, then President Nixon rewarded him with an appointment as ambassador to Great Britain, the nation's premier diplomatic post. Like so many things about Annenberg, this became a cause of controversy and criticism. At the Senate hearings on his nomination, he was asked about his father's conviction and imprisonment, to which he made a revealing reply. "There is no question," he said, "that a tragedy of such magnitude will either destroy you or inspire you to overcome it—and drive you on to deeds of affirmative character."

He was confirmed, and after a stumbling start he performed capably in the post. His term of public service proved to be a watershed, greatly improving his reputation. When the queen of England conferred a knighthood on him a few years later, his respectability was finally and gratifyingly established.

Annenberg had long been a generous giver to charities and educational institutions, but after his return from public service he moved decisively to make philanthropy the primary focus of his life. He began by selling off a good part of his Triangle company, including his newspapers and his broadcasting properties. That transformation was completed after he sold his remaining properties to Australian media magnate Rupert Murdoch for $3.6 billion in 1989.

Annenberg's approach to philanthropy, like almost every other facet of the man, has been subject to controversy—including questioning of his motivation, his methods, and his intentions. But there can be no questioning of his extraordinary generosity from his earliest years. As a starting point in appraising his role as a donor, it is helpful to begin with some facts. Because he has never sought publicity for his gifts, and indeed has been rather secretive about them, no complete list or tally has ever been published. One informed estimate is that Walter Annenberg has already given away the equivalent of some $1.5 billion, is currently distributing more than $30 million a year, and in the coming few years will probably allocate almost a billion more to philanthropy. This places him among the top handful of givers in American history.

There is no trace of the hundreds of small gifts Annenberg has distributed whenever a special need or human tragedy has caught his attention—such as cash awards to employees with serious medical problems, for example, and gifts to the widow of the Dallas policeman slain by Lee Harvey Oswald. These bestowals, among many similar ones, were all done with no fanfare.

While not definitive, the following list includes some of the major donations Walter Annenberg has made over the years:

· A series of million-dollar gifts, given in the name of his mother, Sadie Annenberg, in the 1940s and 1950s, to such organizations as the United Jewish Agencies, the Albert Einstein College of Medicine, New York's Mt. Sinai School of Medicine, and the Sadie Annenberg School of Music.

· $1.5 million for Annenberg Hall at Temple University in Philadelphia.

· $20 million to the Peddie School, which he attended as a teenager.

· Approximately $3 million per year to the Annenberg School of Communications at the University of Pennsylvania, through the Annenberg School at Radnor, Pennsylvania; and comparable amounts to the Annenberg schools of communications at the University of Southern California and Boston's Northeastern University.

· Approximately $6 million to the Annenberg Research Institute for Judaic and Near Eastern Studies in Philadelphia.

· $6 million to the University of Pennsylvania for the construction of the Annenberg Center for Communications Arts and Sciences (plus $2 million for operating costs).

· $150 million in 1981 to create a joint Annenberg–Corporation for Public Broadcasting project to give grants to filmmakers, universities, and public television stations across the nation to produce college-level television courses in video and filmmaking. (The result has been dozens of new program series, including such notable ones as "The Brain, Mind, and Behavior," and "The Constitution, That Delicate Balance.")

· $10 million in the early 1980s to the Eisenhower Medical Center in Palm Springs, California, for the creation of the Annenberg Center for Health Sciences.

· $1.5 million per year for operating expenses to the Annenberg

Washington Program, a research and seminar center to assess how communications policies affect American life.
· His $1 billion art collection given to the New York Metropolitan Museum in 1991.

To carry out his many philanthropic enterprises, Annenberg equipped himself early on with various vehicles through which to distribute his gifts. These included two large foundations—the M. L. Annenberg Foundation in honor of his father and the Annenberg Fund—and the so-called Annenberg School at Radnor, Pennsylvania, which operates as a grant-making foundation.

All in all, Annenberg's record of giving is a formidable one, not only in scale but in innovativeness. For many years both print and broadcast media were regarded by the major American foundations as somehow beneath respect and were ignored. It was not until the period after World War II that a few of the largest foundations began to take an interest, especially in the new electronic media. In the 1960s the Ford Foundation sponsored an experimental program center called the TV Workshop that was influential. A few years later the Carnegie Corporation supported a commission on the educational possibilities of television, an initiative that led directly to the creation of the Public Broadcasting Corporation, after which Ford poured millions of dollars into facilities for the new system. The Markle Foundation also has worked in this field. Thus Annenberg had some philanthropic predecessors, but he has played the major role in creating a set of institutions for training, research, and new-program development in the electronic media. It is he, more than any other donor, who has brought philanthropy into the contemporary media era.

There is some disagreement about the quality of some Annenberg initiatives—the schools at the University of Pennsylvania and at the University of Southern California, for example, and the communications seminars in Washington. There has also been acute concern at times about whether the terms and requirements of the grants made by the Annenberg School at Radnor infringed upon and threatened the integrity of the recipient institutions, but Annenberg's restraint in using the potential for intrusiveness built into the arrangements has now caused such concern largely to disappear.

The distinctive qualities of Walter Annenberg as a philanthropist have been these: He has been strongly motivated to charitable giving since he became rich. He has been a sentimental and impulsive giver, as well as a very skillful and strategic one. Like many of the great givers, he has had something of an "edifice complex"—showing a preference for establishing new operating entities with his name, or his family's name, on them. His giving has been an intensely personal matter, and he has taken a very strong role in defining his interests, conceiving his projects, and maintaining authority over his whole philanthropic program.

Annenberg's most important philanthropic initiatives have originated in an interest or creative idea of his own—in one of "Walter's epiphanies," as his associates have called the remarkably profitable ideas he injected into his companies. He has made use of capable advisors. He has spread his bets over a range of different projects and programs, and he has been a skilled—and often demanding—deal maker with his grantees. He has not sought publicity for his gifts; indeed, he has been publicity-shy, sometimes secretive. He has had confidence in his instincts and has been willing again and again to follow an unorthodox path. He has been, in effect, the kind of determined individualist and entrepreneur in his philanthropy that he was in his business career.

Whatever he set out to prove after his father's death Walter Annenberg has now proven—in business, in public service, and in philanthropy. But his dedication to philanthropy is far from finished. Now in his eighties, he has been moving carefully and decisively to tidy up his affairs, make some additional major gifts, and provide for the continuity of his philanthropy after his eventual death.

In 1989 Annenberg sold his remaining Triangle publications for more than $3 billion. Shortly thereafter he created the Annenberg Foundation as the successor corporation to his Radnor School. According to the brief announcement which has been made, the Annenberg Foundation will fulfill the contractual obligations of the Radnor School for the support of his various other schools and projects, and it will also be a general grant-making foundation, with his wife as vice chair of its board. It will operate in perpetuity, its endowment committed to the educational purposes he has long supported.

Some Comparisons

These three—Lasker, Beckman, and Annenberg—have in common extraordinary records of achievement as philanthropists. But in many other respects they present a mix of contrasts and similarities. Their personalities are very different, as are their fields of interest. They also represent very different scales of wealth.

All three began their philanthropy relatively early in life and developed their experience and skills as donors gradually. All have worked hard at philanthropy, giving it the full benefit of their energy and ideas. All have been very personal, hands-on donors, conceiving their own programs and deciding on their major gifts. On the whole, all three have relied essentially on their own instincts, judgment, and ideas in distributing their gifts, rather than on a large professional staff.

Mrs. Lasker was a crusader, a missionary in the cause of health. Beckman, scientist and entrepreneur, has been committed to the cause of science, and he has been brilliantly selective in his gifts, targeting them on explorations at the frontiers of knowledge. And he has been innovative and realistic in delegating to a great scientific university, Cal Tech, the responsibility for carrying on his kind of grant making after his death.

Both Mary Lasker and Annenberg in their grant making reflect the profound changes in American life since the days of Rockefeller, Carnegie, and Rosenwald, especially the immensely greater roles of Washington and the media as power centers in national affairs. Annenberg, with his own background in the media, has for the first time made modern communications policy the central focus of a major philanthropic program. Mary Lasker, in waging her crusade against the dreaded killer diseases, masterfully used all the modern techniques of mass communications, lobbying, and networking, as well as the leverage of her relatively modest resources, to redirect governmental policies and budgets.

Beckman and Annenberg, however, given the scale of their wealth, have been indifferent to leveraging and have been more inclined to hedge their bets by funding a variety of existing institutions.

Yet, with their various interests, styles, and personal abilities, all three donors had a significant impact on American life and deserve to rank among our greatest philanthropists.

Chapter Five

—◦°₂§~°§—

The New Super-Rich (A Diverse Quartet)

Warren Buffett, Bill Gates, Leslie Wexner, and George Soros

The four men who are probably the richest individuals in the United States today are similar in their capacity to accumulate wealth, but radically different in their propensity to give some of it away and in their skill in doing so.

The four are Warren Buffett of Omaha, Nebraska, number one in *Forbes* magazine's ranking of the richest Americans; Bill Gates, of Microsoft; Leslie Wexner of Ohio, a major clothing chain owner; and George Soros, an international financier. Buffett's and Gates's fortunes are currently estimated to be over $8 billion each. Soros' wealth is in that vicinity and growing at an estimated $1 billion a year. Wexner's holdings, already over $2 billion, are also growing rapidly.

Buffett has indicated one or two broad areas of interest in philanthropy, but despite the fact he is now in his sixties, he has done nothing yet of any consequence in either area.

Gates, not yet forty and just recently married, is deeply engaged in developing his already huge computer software company, Microsoft. He expects to give the bulk of his fortune to philanthropy eventually, but as of now, philanthropy will have to wait.

Wexner is in his late fifties, single, and childless. Beginning with one dress shop in Columbus, Ohio, thirty years ago, his chain, The Limited, now operates some 3,900 stores nationwide, plus a booming direct-mail catalog business. Whether Buffett will ever emerge as a generous or interesting donor is doubtful. Gates is still young and preoccupied with building his company, but he could someday be an intriguing new factor in philanthropy. Wexner, in contrast, already shows extraordinary promise. As soon as his fortune began to accumulate, his charitable activities began, and he is now emerging as one of the very large, active, and effective donors in the United States. It is quite unlikely, however, that any of them will even approximate the achievements of Soros, who by his creativity, courage, and commitment, is well on the way to making himself one of the historic figures in this field.

These four make a dramatic and thought-provoking set of contrasts.

Warren Buffett

Warren Buffett is an icon among American investment managers, with a sustained record of success that is phenomenal. An investor who placed $10,000 in his investment vehicle, Berkshire Hathaway, in 1950 would have been worth about $65 million in 1994. So Buffett is understandably revered by his beneficiaries. And because of his salty and candid commentaries on all kinds of public issues, he is also regarded as something of a sage.

As a money giver rather than a money maker, however, Buffett is monumentally less impressive. His principal initiative in philanthropy has been to assess every shareholder in Berkshire Hathaway an amount per share to be given to charity. The shareholders, who are willingly deprived of this small portion of their annual gains, then can choose the charities to which their assessment is sent.

Warren and Susan Buffett designate his foundation to receive their annual allocation, currently some $5 million, which the foundation subsequently distributes in grants. *Forbes* magazine estimates that Mr. Buffett has produced an annual return for Berkshire Hathaway shares of 29 percent annually for the past twenty-three years and that the Buffetts' current holdings are valued at more than $8 billion. If this is correct, his annual return is currently on the order of $2.3 billion, and $5 million of annual gifts is something less than .025 percent of his annual gains from his Berkshire Hathaway holdings alone. This then is a measure of the pinchpenny annual charitable giving of the wealthiest man in the nation.

Warren Buffett's abstention from a larger philanthropic effort is justified by a spokesman on the grounds that for him to sell or otherwise donate any of his Berkshire Hathaway shares would "seriously impair his ability to run and grow Berkshire Hathaway." In effect, as a matter of personal policy Buffett refuses to take those steps—namely, to make gifts of additional cash or stock to his foundation—that would permit an increase in the scale of his giving. When asked why Buffett does not turn more of his attention and energies to philanthropy, the same spokesman stated that "he simply enjoys what he does too much to do something else."

From a broader national perspective, this minimalist policy

sends the message to the wealthy class in the United States—who hold Mr. Buffett in the highest esteem for his investment skills—that the richest one of them all sees no urgency and places no priority on mounting a serious philanthropic effort during his active years. This is hardly the kind of philanthropic leadership that might be hoped for.

Such a stance on the part of Mr. Buffett is particularly strange because he has repeatedly declared that his primary philanthropic objective will be to do something about the world population explosion. As a master of investment strategy, he is well aware of the power of exponential curves. He must therefore be well aware that world population is now on a dangerously rapid exponential growth curve. The longer he waits to activate his philanthropy, the more grave and irreversible the world population problem becomes and the further and further behind the curve his potential philanthropic impact must fall.

If he continues to proceed on the optimistic assumption that he still has a long, active life ahead of him, that there is plenty of time to get around to serious philanthropy, and that launching a major foundation that will carry on an effective program and be faithful to his goals is an easy task, then Warren Buffett is taking a wild gamble with fate—a risk that he would surely call reckless and stupid if it were a business judgment.

Bill Gates

Another super-rich American who may someday be a heavyweight in philanthropy—but who at present is still totally preoccupied with the development of his company—is William H. Gates III of Seattle, Washington.

A onetime Harvard dropout, he is founder, chief executive, and the largest shareholder of Microsoft, the largest computer software company in the world. As the second wealthiest American (after Warren Buffett) his fortune is currently in the range of $8 billion and still growing rapidly.

In his late thirties and recently married, Gates talked candidly with an interviewer from *Playboy* magazine in 1994 about his attitudes toward money and the eventual use of his wealth. He is not extravagant, and he expects to remain very active with his company for at least another ten years. Then, in his fifties, he expects to begin giving away some 95 percent of his fortune to charitable and scientific purposes. "It's a lot to give away and it's going to take time," he told his interviewer.

When asked about heirs, Gates commented, "I don't believe in burdening any children I might have with too much wealth. They'll have enough. They'll be comfortable."

Then this exchange:

Playboy. You'll give them only a billion, maybe?

   Gates. No, no—are you kidding? Nothing like that. One percent of that. . . .

Playboy. So you want them to be as self-made as you?

   Gates. No, that's not the point. The point is that ridiculous sums of money can be confusing. . . . I'm very well grounded because of my parents and my job and what I believe in. Some people ask me why I don't own a plane, for instance. Why? Because you can get used to that kind of stuff, and I think that's bad. It takes you away from normal experiences in a way that is probably debilitating. So I control that kind of thing intentionally. . . . So I'm in the same traffic as everybody else. I sit in the same coach seat as everybody else. . . .

Playboy.   Does privilege corrupt?

Gates.   It can. It's easy to get spoiled by things that alienate you from what is important.

If Bill Gates can continue to resist getting spoiled by his wealth and becoming alienated from what is important, if he can demonstrate some of the creativity in his philanthropy that he has shown in his business, and if he does not wait too long to get started, he could be one of the great new American philanthropists of the early twenty-first century.

Leslie Wexner

Leslie Wexner, who learned early to be charitable from his immigrant parents, began his giving as soon as his fortune began to grow, starting with gifts to his home city, Columbus, and his home state, Ohio.

Characteristically, Wexner has not only given money but has also helped raise it, serving on a number of charity boards and helping nonprofits with their strategic planning. For the Columbus United Way, for example, he helped develop an innovative plan that has quadrupled the rate of giving to the organization in recent years.

Wexner has also been active as a civic leader in Columbus, directing efforts to improve the airport and the commercial development of the central city. With his mother, Bella, he created the Wexner Foundation in 1973. Through it he has given some $25 million to establish an avant garde arts center at Ohio State University, and an additional $6 million to set up a system of regional science centers in the state. He has made a large gift to expand the research capabilities of the Columbus Children's Hospital, and he has loaned several million dollars to build Wexner Heritage Village, a Jewish retirement community in the city.

Nationally, Wexner has made major gifts to the United Jewish Appeal, the United Negro College Fund, Harvard University, and the Whitney Museum of American Art.

In 1991 Wexner broke new ground, creating the Ohio Higher Education Trust, a grant-making foundation to which he made a gift of $250 million. This action moved him into the ranks of the nation's megagivers, and it may be only the first of his major initiatives.

Wexner's style of giving is already quite distinctive. Those in the nonprofit sector who have worked with him call him "a visionary, an intellectual giver," and "a motivator of others." He has never sought publicity or public acclaim for his giving; indeed, he has sought to avoid it. "It's very comfortable to give privately; it's a little embarrassing to give publicly," he has said. "But when you give publicly, and when you're giving for the right reasons in terms of setting examples, believing that sharing your experience with others will influence them in a positive way, then I think it's very appropriate."

For Wexner, "One of the most pleasant characteristics of mankind is the ability to care about other beings that you don't know." He does not believe in "giving until it hurts." His measure of successful giving is, "When I make a gift, do I really feel terrific? If I don't feel terrific, I know I haven't given enough," he says.

At his age, and with his fortune, Wexner's philanthropy has probably only just begun. He says his goal is to use his wealth productively in behalf of society: "The way to think about giving in general is, you never know when your lease expires. I'd like to feel that I've always met my obligations, personal ones and community ones. I'd like to check out with 10 cents and have seen the good happen while I was on earth."

George Soros

Probably the boldest and most visionary major donor in the world at the present time is George Soros, a Hungarian-born international financier. In the early 1940s he escaped the Holocaust by fleeing to Britain. He has since become an American citizen and made New York City his headquarters.

In the course of the past twenty years Soros has become immensely rich and hugely and creatively philanthropic. In that period he has undertaken through his philanthropy nothing less than to open up the once-closed Communist societies of Eastern Europe to a free flow of ideas and scientific knowledge from the outside world.

In one of his first undertakings more than a decade ago, Soros launched a number of projects to expose some of the able young men and women of his native Hungary to intellectual and scientific freedom. As he persuaded their government to accept the conditions he attached to his grants, his intent was not only to help individuals but also to stir discontent and ultimately to destabilize the Communist government. Within a short period that began to occur.

But by that time Communist control was collapsing throughout Eastern Europe and all the regions of the Soviet Union, and Soros moved quickly to focus his philanthropy on helping those struggling societies make an orderly transition to a radically changed political, economic, and intellectual environment. An important part of that heroic effort has been to pour hundreds of millions of dollars into a multinational effort to salvage the scientific traditions and the leading scientists of Eastern Europe from a possible total social and economic collapse.

In less than a decade Soros funded foundations in twenty-two countries, including nineteen former Communist nations. These grants include

· $6 million annually to the Soros Foundation, Hungary, for cultural and educational activities

· $27 million annually to foundations in the former Soviet republics for education reform, training of public administrators, and privatization institutes

· $25 million over five years to the Central European University established in 1990 in Prague and Budapest

· $50 million to the Soros Humanitarian Foundation for Bosnia and Herzegovina for assistance to victims of the war in the Balkans

• $15 million over three years for the Open Society Foundation to promote human rights and civil liberties in South Africa

· $100 million for two years to his new International Science Foundation to support scientific research in the former Soviet Union. Soros wants this foundation to serve as a sort of Noah's Ark preserving at least part of the USSR's scientific tradition, which is now being threatened by the economic troubles there.

· $15 million to a new research institute in Prague to analyze the political, social, and economic transformation of Eastern Europe and the former Soviet Union, and to train journalists and policy analysts from those areas.

In one of his rare failures, the Soros Foundation attempted a few years ago to enter mainland China with an offer to establish some twenty public reading rooms throughout the country, each stocked with scientific and scholarly journals from various non-Communist countries. At the beginning, Beijing seemed ready to cooperate. But in the end the regime decided the idea was too dangerous and the foundation had to withdraw. Soros candidly admits that the failure was due to his "misunderstanding the historical moment" in that country.

By the scope of his vision, the scale of his commitments, and the courage and creativity of his initiatives, Soros already ranks with the greatest American philanthropists ever. His international efforts constitute a heroic chapter in the history of philanthropy—in terms of creativity, courage, timeliness, and scale of commitment. Not since Rockefeller and Carnegie has such a force been seen in the field of donorship.

A caveat: The massiveness of Soros's grants in Eastern Europe and the chaotic condition of those reemerging states have involved him increasingly with their heads of government and other key political figures. There is evidence that as time has passed he has been drawn, or has pushed himself, into matters beyond the proper boundaries of philanthropy—such as his efforts in support of the creation of a new "Macedonian" state in the Balkans. It would be a great tragedy if such hubris should dim his brilliant philanthropic record thus far.

Some Comparisons and Contrasts

How do these four big newcomers on the philanthropic scene compare in their approaches and potential impact with the three historic greats, Rockefeller, Carnegie, and Rosenwald? There are a few interesting similarities and some striking differences.

All the earlier giants began their philanthropy while still in their active years. Among the newcomers, Soros and Wexner are the only ones now following that pattern.

All the old greats had a strong sense of mission, and the scope of their interests was broadly national and even international. Rockefeller was a bold, visionary, entrepreneurial launcher of new programs and new institutions, several of them global in scope.

Carnegie was equally sweeping in his interests and creative in his institutional creations. He also had a strong interest in the promotion of international peace and the then nascent League of Nations. Rosenwald's philanthropy was highly entrepreneurial and primarily national in scope. But he also had a strong concern for the welfare of the Jewish community internationally. Because he was not a Zionist, some of these initiatives got him into controversy.

Buffett and Gates are still undefined and inactive potential large donors. Whether their philanthropy will ever be sizable, creative, and influential remains to be seen.

Of the two who are active and creative, Wexner is a donor somewhat in the style of Rosenwald, with strong personal involvement in his giving and keen interests in the development of his own locality and in Jewish welfare. Beyond that, his interests seem to be focused more on higher education than on race relations and the poor. But his career in philanthropy is still evolving, and where it may ultimately take him is impossible at this point to predict.

Soros is a donor more on the Rockefeller model—bold, entrepreneurial, and global in the reach of his objectives. He already takes rank with the greatest donors of the past in the scale of his giving, the scope of his objectives, and the boldness and creativity of his initiatives.

He is passionately devoted to the idea of Europe as an open, democratic society "not dominated by the state or by any particular ideology; where nobody has a monopoly on truth; where minorities and minority opinions are respected." He is also committed to advancing the process of European integration. In the pursuit of that sweeping objective, he has shown a masterful sense of timing and a brilliant sense of the historical moment; and he has already made an astonishing series of huge, creative grants throughout both Western and Eastern Europe.

In some respects Soros even outranks his great predecessors: Rockefeller was a great industrial entrepreneur on a worldwide scale, but his philanthropies were separate from his business activities; neither directly influenced the other. Likewise, Carnegie's business activities had no relationship to his philanthropies—other than generating the funds that supported them. Soros is different in that he is an active participant in the economic (and to some degree the political) processes that are powerful elements in determining whether democratic patterns and economic and political integration evolve in Europe. In his business activities he is able "to move markets" by the timing and scale of his actions. He can and has forced the revaluation of European currencies and overpowered the policies of central banks, with massive impacts on the processes of integration or disintegration of the European Community. He is well aware of and candid about this, saying that it creates opportunities for him as a major investor and also imposes restraints and responsibilities because of the interaction of his philanthropic and his financial initiatives (see George Soros, "The Prospects for European Disintegration," *Aspen Institute Quarterly*, Summer 1994).

Rockefeller's international business activities, though huge, had no evident connection with his philanthropic initiatives. Andrew Carnegie, in addition to his philanthropic efforts in behalf of international peace, carried on an active correspondence with various world leaders in support of that cause. But to the extent he had any influence on the course of events—which is unclear—it was as a respected private citizen, and not one who wielded economic power over such matters.

George Soros, however, has both a driving philanthropic mission and significant economic power to bring to bear on the actual course of world events. If he exercises all that influence skillfully and constructively, he might even surpass the achievements of the greatest of his predecessors.

Part Three

—⚜—

The Rising Role
of Women

Chapter Six

—⚬⸏⸐⚬—

The Forgotten History

In the past, and indeed until quite recent times, the general impression prevailed in the United States that, although women have long been active in charitable work—the "lady bountiful" image—philanthropy in its most substantial and creative sense was essentially a male preserve.

This is a serious and a curious misperception. It is now generally recognized that women along with men have been in the forefront of all the important national social movements of the past—abolition of slavery, health care and hospital reform, prison reform, public education, social programs for children and the poor, Prohibition, women's suffrage, and many others. From Susan B. Anthony, Harriet Tubman, Jane Addams, and Clara Barton to Eleanor Roosevelt, they form a distinguished line of leaders who have made major contributions to the constitutional, institutional, and social development of the country.

But it has yet to be understood that, in addition to all their volunteer work and charitable service, they have been important figures in the development of American foundations and philanthropy. Let a representative few of them, then, pass in parade:

Sophia Smith (1796–1870) inherited her family's fortune at age sixty-five. She carefully considered putting it into a school for the deaf (she had become deaf at the age of forty), but then decided that the general education of women was a more urgent concern. So she founded the notable Smith College in Massachusetts with an endowment of some $390,000.

Sarah Platt Haines Doremus (1802–1877) was born into a New York City family long active in charitable work. She married a wealthy merchant, Thomas C. Doremus, and thereafter was able to undertake a wide variety of philanthropic projects. In 1828 she organized the collection of supplies for the relief of Greek women suffering under Turkish oppression. In the 1830s she became interested in prison reform, and eventually she became the national director of the Women's Prison Association. In 1850 she helped establish the New York House and School of Industry, where women were given useful work and where instruction was given to poor children too ill clad to attend school. In 1854 Doremus was among the founders of the Nursery and Child's Hospital, where medical and day care were provided to needy children. Among the other causes to which she gave her energy and funds were the Presbyterian Home for Aged Women and relief for victims of the Irish famine.

Margaret Gaffney Haughery (1813–82) was born in Ireland and was brought to the United States by her immigrant parents in

1818. She received no schooling and never learned to read or write. When she was five, her parents died in a yellow fever epidemic in Baltimore. She spent the next several years working as a servant girl. In 1835 she married Charles Haughery, and they moved to New Orleans. He died in the following year, and she, after working for a time as a laundress in a hotel, used her meager savings to buy a pair of cows and start a dairy. She was soon a welcome sight on the streets of the city, where she peddled—and often gave away—milk.

Despite, or because of, her generosity, Haughery prospered, and by 1840 she had a herd of forty dairy cows. In that year she contributed funds to the Sisters of Charity to help them open the New Orleans Female Orphan Asylum. In the years that followed ten more such institutions were assisted by her benefactions, most notably the St. Vincent's Orphan Asylum.

In addition, Haughery was ready to give her help to the city in other ways, particularly as a nurse during the yellow fever epidemics that regularly struck the region.

In 1858 Haughery acquired a small bakery as payment of a debt. She gave up her dairy, expanded the bakery, and soon proved herself a master of business. Hers was the first bakery in the city to use the new steam technology, and she introduced the idea of selling packaged crackers. After a few years of such innovations, her enterprise become one of the largest in the city.

During the Civil War Haughery directed her charitable efforts especially toward soldiers' families. Her personal benefactions were done with unassuming humility, and much of her work in that sphere was unknown to the public during her lifetime. When she died in 1882, leaving an estate of nearly half a million dollars, she bequeathed most of it to Catholic, Protestant, and Jewish charities.

In July 1884 a statue of her, bought by public subscription, was unveiled in Margaret Haughery Park in New Orleans.

Catherine Wolfe Bruce (1816–1900) inherited her wealth from her father, a prominent publisher. Well-educated and traveled, she became a patron of astronomical and astrophysical research. Although little known to the public, she was well known and greatly admired in scientific circles for her significant support of research in this field.

Anna Jeanes (1822–1907) was the daughter of a wealthy Philadelphia Quaker family. After inheriting the family fortune, she spent the remaining years of her life giving it away. Her pioneering efforts to increase and improve education in rural elementary schools in the South for both black and white children laid the groundwork for the later and larger programs of Rockefeller's General Education Board.

When Jeanes died in 1907, she distributed the remainder of her wealth in several large bequests to various schools and hospitals. The bequest that brought the most attention was a large gift to Swarthmore College, for it contained the condition that the school give up intercollegiate athletics. Presumably she had football in mind, for she is reputed to have remarked about football players, "They must be ungodly men who mimic war when there is peace."

Ellen Collins (1828–1912), daughter of a wealthy Quaker family in New York, was an active abolitionist and a very practical social reformer. Dismayed by the miserable tenement areas of the city, she acquired and rehabilitated slum properties to demonstrate the good influence a responsible landlord could have over the lives of the poor.

Ellen Browning Scripps (1836–1932) began her career as a journalist in a newspaper started by her brother in Detroit, Michigan.

Over the years he developed a chain of newspapers in which she was both a collaborator and investor. She never married, and when she was in her sixties and independently wealthy, she moved to California and devoted herself to distributing her fortune to worthy causes. Among her most notable initiatives were the creation of the Scripps Institute of Oceanography and the Scripps Clinic and Research Foundation for Bio-medical Research. She also founded Scripps College for Women in Claremont, California.

Scripps had a lively interest in political and social ideas. In a gift she made to establish a recreation center in the town of La Jolla, California, she specified that it should be maintained for the discussion of public questions and that no speaker should be barred because of his opinions. She vigorously opposed the "deportation delirium" of Attorney General Mitchell Palmer after World War I and took an active part in early efforts to abolish the death penalty.

Bernice Pauahi Bishop (1836–84) was a Hawaiian princess who broke tradition by marrying a young American, Charles Bishop, who was then working in Honolulu. A member of the royal Kamehameha family, she later inherited its vast land holdings. At her death she left nearly all her property—some 10 percent of the total land area of the islands, now valued in the hundreds of millions of dollars—in trust to establish the Bishop Museum (an outstanding Polynesian ethnological institution) and to build and maintain two schools for children of Hawaiian ancestry. Each of the five trustees of Bishop's estate now receives $750,000 annually in fees. Because of the extraordinary influence of the estate in Hawaiian affairs, political charges periodically swirl around her great endowment.

Olivia Phelps-Stokes (1847–1927) and her sister Caroline were daughters of a fervently religious Quaker family in New York. Their father, a prominent merchant and banker, had many charitable interests, and headed the New York Colonization Society, which helped establish the Republic of Liberia for freed American slaves. After the deaths of their parents the two daughters dedicated their lives and their inheritance to a wide range of causes—the YWCA, various missionary efforts, homes for the aged and infirm, and most notably the advancement of black education, especially vocational education, in the South. The sisters left their wealth to establish the Phelps-Stokes Fund to improve housing for the poor in New York and for the education of blacks in the South. The fund still exists as a reputable organization working in behalf of blacks and for improved relations among the races.

Elizabeth Milbank Anderson (1850–1921) was the daughter of a wealthy New York banker who left her a large part of his estate when he died in 1884. After distributing gifts for various causes in the following years, she created the Milbank Memorial in 1905 to do research in epidemiology and nutrition. It has subsequently supported programs to create neighborhood health centers, to help European orphans and needy children, and to address the health and safety needs of migrant workers. The fund continues as a highly respected private operating foundation.

Mary Elizabeth Garrett (1854–1915) belonged to a wealthy merchant and railroad family and made singular contributions in the field of education. In funding a girls' school in Baltimore, she required that its students pass an entrance examination for a college of the highest rank in order to graduate—an innovation that affected schools throughout the nation. She also made large gifts for the development of Bryn Mawr College for women and was an important donor to the women's suffrage movement. Her most innovative and powerful action, however, was to make a large funding commitment in 1899 for the creation of the Johns Hopkins Medical School. She did this with two key conditions: that it admit women on the same basis as men and that it be a graduate school of medicine, none of which existed in the United States at that time. A few years later, when the Rockefeller Foundation was launching its historic program to reform American medical schools, the example of Hopkins was the pivot on which that great initiative turned.

Kate Macy Ladd (1863–1945) was the daughter of a Quaker family with a long tradition in philanthropy. Her father left her a trust fund of Standard Oil shares which—as their value increased—provided her with the means of greatly increasing her benefactions. Medical services were a strong interest, and Ladd made many grants to hospitals in New York, Philadelphia, and elsewhere. Her major action, however, was the creation in 1930 of the Josiah Macy Jr. Foundation in honor of her father. Before doing so, she commissioned a well-known professor of medicine, Ludwig Kast, to make a two-year survey of philanthropy in American. Since Kast's study concluded that foundations were neglecting scientific research, that then became the focus of the Macy Foundation's work, especially research into medical problems that bore a relationship to other fields such as biology and the social sciences. The Macy Foundation, having built a solid reputation, now concentrates on programs in medical education and the training of minorities in medicine.

Carrie Bamberger Fuld (1864–1944) was born into a family that developed one of the nation's largest department stores. She and her brother sold the enterprise in the 1920s for $25 million, shortly before the Great Crash of the stock market. Thereafter they devoted themselves to philanthropy. Their first idea was to establish a new medical school in New Jersey, but after consulting with Abraham Flexner, the notable Rockefeller advisor, they were persuaded to create a new institute in the field of general scholarship and science, resembling the Rockefeller Institute for Medical Research. So the two of them joined in founding the Institute for Advanced Studies in Princeton, New Jersey. It opened in 1933 with Albert Einstein as its head. Almost immediately it became a world-renowned intellectual center, and its preeminence continues to this day.

Ima Hogg (1882–1975) was born in Texas, the favorite child of a very successful businessman and politician, James Stephen Hogg, who in the late nineteenth century served as a four-term governor of the state. He had the greatest trust in her character and judgment, and from a very early age she played an important role in all his activities. After his death in 1906, she put the family's wealth and political connections to use in a variety of civic and philanthropic projects. One of her major interests was mental health, and in the 1930s she conceived the idea of providing mental-health services throughout the state through the University of Texas. This led to the creation and funding of what is now known as the Hogg Foundation for Mental Health, an outstanding research institution at that university. She also founded the Houston Child Guidance Center, a pioneering center in child psychiatry.

Ima Hogg also had an interest in music. She played a major role in organizing the Houston Symphony and served as its president for many years. Another of her interests was historic preservation, a somewhat unusual taste at the time in a state consumed by the ideal of economic growth. Among her several projects in this field, the most notable was her endowment of Bayou Bend, her home for nearly forty years, which, with its fine gardens, she gave to the Houston Museum of Fine Arts in 1966 with funds for its maintenance. It contains a large and carefully researched assemblage of American antiques and furnishings.

Last in this cavalcade of women philanthropists from the nine-teenth century is one who in many respects should rank first, Margaret Olivia Slocum Sage (1828–1918). Hers was the first major foundation created by an American woman. It incorporated the best thinking of the time about building flexibility into a foundation's program and broadening the role of the trustees. And not only was it infused with Mrs. Sage's strong convictions about its mission but also it incorporated important new ideas about using research findings on social problems as a basis for instituting reforms. In many respects Margaret Sage's approach to philanthropic donorship foreshadowed some of the more significant trends in American philanthropy in the twentieth century.

Mrs. Sage was a woman with a good social pedigree from upstate New York. She graduated from Emma Willard's Female Academy in 1847, taught school for twenty-two years, and in midlife married Russell Sage, a widower from New York City. A very wealthy businessman, Sage did not believe in charity. Indeed he was regularly vilified and mocked as a miser; a cruel, heartless usurer; and a corrupter of politicians and the judiciary. Many maintained that he possessed no human feelings and that he was a "charitable bankrupt." Whether or not this characterization was true, his second wife had very different inclinations, and after her husband's death in 1906 she quickly emerged as a new kind of American philanthropist. By the terms of his will, she inherited some $63 million. This, according to newspaper accounts at the time, made her the richest woman in America. She immediately set to work to establish and endow a new foundation to be named, ironically, in his honor.

Margaret Sage was a champion of women's rights and, perhaps confirmed by her marital experience, she believed that women as the moral superiors of men were primarily responsible for the moral progress of civilization. She also had a driving determination to do something to improve the social and living conditions of the poor in the United States. The problem of indiscriminate and purely ameliorative giving was an important concern of hers. She determined to do something about the causes of pauperism rather than simply distribute funds to alleviate individual suffering.

In designing the legal form of her foundation, Sage and her lawyer, who had broad experience in philanthropy, agreed that a philanthropic trust "should be elastic in form and method to work in different ways at different times" for the permanent improvement of social conditions in the United States. Together they drafted a charter for a foundation that was unusual for its open-endedness of purpose and for its explicit public-policy orientation.

Mrs. Sage then committed $10 million to the new entity, and it was promptly chartered in 1907. There were just eight foundations existing in the country at that time, only two of which had a capital fund equal to that of the new Sage Foundation, and no other was active in the field in which it would operate. Its declared objectives were nothing less than to formulate and facilitate the reform of American social, economic, and political life. These ends were to be achieved by promoting surveys of social conditions, making their findings available to influential citizens, and mobilizing public opinion to bring about change.

In that hopeful, far-gone day, the new idea of using science to solve the problems of society was greeted with great enthusiasm. The newspapers in New York and other cities immediately acclaimed the fledgling foundation for the breadth and boldness of its aims, for the degree of discretion permitted to its trustees, and for the size of its endowment: "One of the most significant gifts in all modern philanthropy," said one paper; "Its managers will not be tied down to any outgrown subject of inquiry or belief," said another. Such was the tenor of the accolades the Russell Sage Foundation received.

The foundation got underway quickly, hiring a good staff and commissioning significant studies. Over the years the quality of the work it sponsored and the impact of its studies on social-welfare policy and legislation were considerable. It became a highly respected research and public policy center, the first of its kind. The basic processes it fostered—bringing together academic experts, influential private groups, and government to launch initiatives on problems ranging from housing to child care to welfare reform and (especially) the problems of working women—were a major and influential innovation. The Brookings Institution and the Twentieth Century Fund were among the think tanks built on its model a decade later.

Margaret Sage remained actively involved in the foundation's planning and programs until her death in 1918, ten years after its founding. After the death of Mrs. Sage, its activities gradually became more focused on academic concerns than on activist social reform. Giving grants to organizations such as the Social Science Research Council and the National Bureau of Economic Research, as well as to many university centers, the Russell Sage Foundation has had great impact on the research priorities of those institutions and on the growth of new disciplines, particularly in the social sciences. Although it has lost the activist spirit of its founder, it has been a durable creation, and it continues to be held in high esteem by many elements of the academic community.

Margaret Sage was representative of the outstanding nineteenth and early-twentieth-century women who were not only generous donors but also individuals guided by a highly developed concept of effective philanthropy. For example, Anna Jeanes, in all her giving, emphasized the pursuit of long-term goals and concentrated on projects that would develop competence and self-sufficiency rather than providing mere palliative aid. Elizabeth Milbank Anderson was likewise skeptical of charity that dealt merely with symptoms, not causes—hence her interest in basic scientific research. Her gifts for children's aid and community health centers were intended simply "to provide interim help until government agencies were prepared to assume these responsibilities."

Other women donors shared this recognition of the linkages between private charity and government policy, and of private action as a spur to governmental response. Kate Macy Ladd, for example, believed that "in an enlightened democracy, private philanthropy could best serve by investing in new ideas from which may gradually emerge social functions which in turn should be taken over by and maintained by the public."

A Major Second-Phase Transformation

These summary accounts of the work and ideas of a noble procession of American women philanthropists can do little more than suggest the range and variety of their contributions to an important national tradition, contributions that have been far too little recognized. Their history has somehow been largely overlooked or forgotten.

The brief biographies here are focused on the role of women as donors, as the creators of foundations. There is, however, another important aspect of the participation of women in philanthropy that somehow has been obscured—and that in recent decades has been going through rapid, even revolutionary change. That is their role as philanthropic professionals—as program directors and, increasingly, as senior officers and chief executives of foundations.

It was for a very long time a curious anomaly in the culture of American philanthropy that women were generally acknowledged to be compassionate, caring, nurturing, and oftentimes reformist forces in American life. But in the field of foundations, the officers and professional staffing of those institutions dedicated largely to charitable, educational, and reformist objectives were until well after World War II an almost exclusively male preserve.

Over the past forty years, however, a profound change has occurred. Women are now a rapidly growing presence in the professional and, to some extent, the executive ranks of American foundations. The same change has happened in the leadership of the professional organizations serving the field of philanthropy, such as the Council on Foundations, Independent Sector, and others.

This quiet but massive revolution is ongoing. It represents not only a quantitative shift in the balance, or imbalance, of the roles and influence of men and women in philanthropy and other nonprofit activities, but quite possibly it also portends a qualitative shift in the spirit and future priorities of philanthropy as well.

Women have now demonstrated beyond all possibility of doubt that, given the opportunity, they can organize and administer philanthropic enterprises as capably as men. As donors that has long been evident. In more recent times the movement of women into philanthropy as senior executives and as key program directors is a huge and relatively rapid change that remains too little recognized.

Only a generation ago, and through the period of World War II, there may have been a considerable number of significant women donors, but there were still virtually no places for women in the key executive and professional ranks in foundations. But now many, perhaps most, of the leading foundations have at least one woman on their board, and several, such as the Duke Endowment, have a woman in the chair. Today some of the most outstanding figures in the executive ranks of philanthropy in recent years are women. Among the most notable are Margaret Mahoney, head of the Commonwealth Fund; Elizabeth McCormack, senior advisor on philanthropy to the Rockefeller family; Rebecca Rimel, head of the huge Pew Memorial Trust; Barbara Finberg, executive vice president of Carnegie; Terry Tinson Saario, president of the Northwest Area Foundation; Deborah Leff, head of the Joyce Foundation; Janice Kreamer, head of the Kansas City Community Foundation; Barbara Blum, head of the New York Community Foundation; and Susan Berresford, who has been chosen as successor to Franklin Thomas as head of the Ford Foundation, the nation's largest.

Equally remarkable have been the program directors who have made their names legendary, such as Marcia Thompson, in the Ford Foundation's programs for the arts, and Siobhan Oppenheimer Nicolau, in that foundation's program for Hispanics, Indians, and other minorities.

In the collective organizations of philanthropy, women have also made a great impact. Some of the most outstanding are Virginia Hodginson, research director of Independent Sector, the umbrella organization for nonprofits; Elizabeth Boris, head of the Non-profit Sector Research Fund; Sarah Englehart, head of the Foundation Center; and Kimberly Dennis, director of the Philanthropy Roundtable. Other important and influential figures are Stacy Palmer, executive editor of the *Chronicle of Philanthropy,* and Anne Morgan, once head of the Kerr Foundation and now an advisor to many donors and foundations.

These women are all of the highest capability and standing in their fields, and following on their heels is a still larger new generation of young and able women professionals. As a result of this quiet but radical transformation of the philanthropic professions from an almost exclusively male preserve a relatively short time ago, the philanthropic field is well on its way to having a balanced mix of men and women in key leadership posts.

Access and acceptance women have now gained, and executive and professional ability they have conclusively proved. The deeper question remains whether, by their rise in influence and authority, they are bringing a special dimension of sensitivity and compassion into the institutions and practices of philanthropy that is different from and more relevant to its tasks than that of their male predecessors.

For example, there is an emerging national awareness of the profound meaning and essentiality of the idea of family, of the responsibility of each generation to nurture the next, and of the disastrous consequences for individuals and society if those factors are demeaned or lost.

In this regard it remains a widely held view that women by nature and life experience are on the whole better fitted than men for the tasks of nurturing and teaching children, keeping families together, and providing compassionate services to the needy and the disabled. So it now seems entirely possible that the feminization of philanthropy may make its institutions far more attuned to the contemporary needs of American society than it has ever been before.

In any case, the changes that have taken place will continue to extend the role and influence of women in philanthropy in the coming century. They constitute a fundamental and possibly transforming development.

Chapter Seven

—◦⸙ℰ⸙◦—

Women
in Philanthropy
The Bright Prospect

Historically the shape and focus of American philanthropy has evolved from decade to decade with the shifts in American society and its problems and priorities. None of the changes in the past have exceeded in scale and rapidity the vast transformation of the role of women in every aspect of American life—political, economic, and social—in recent decades. Those changes are rapidly penetrating the entire nonprofit sector at the present time, including philanthropy. The impact is being felt in different ways and in differing degrees in philanthropy's several segments.

First, in the broad territory of charitable and voluntary service, women as organizers, fund-raisers, and service providers have long been a mainstay of the system. Traditionally such activities have provided women one of their most available means of expressing their concerns, pursuing meaningful careers, and performing public service. It can be anticipated that this vast field, including hundreds of thousands of churches, hospitals, schools, and cultural institutions, will continue to offer such outlets in the future. It is too massive and too diverse to change rapidly. But it is changing; and in the future women will clearly hold far more senior-executive and policy-making positions than in the past.

Second, in the sphere of traditional women's organizations—the Junior League, the Girl Scouts, the YWCA, B'nai Brith, and the like—great changes have already occurred. Once regarded as conservative, white, middle- and upper-class enclaves, many local units have now overhauled and greatly invigorated their programs under a new generation of women leaders. To a remarkable degree they have made them more relevant to contemporary problems and attitudes of women and girls of all backgrounds and all classes—introducing programs ranging from vocational training to battered-women's shelters.

Third, such long-established women's social-action organizations as the League of Women Voters and Planned Parenthood have become much more activist and influential in national life than ever before, and their leaders have become national figures. From the reform of presidential debates and the national electoral system to abortion and women's reproductive rights, they have become engaged in some of the most controversial and fundamental issues facing the nation.

In addition, a noteworthy development in recent years has been the establishment of major new activist nonprofits by a new generation of remarkable women. Among the more prominent examples are the Children's Defense Fund, headed by Marian Wright Edelman; the Women's Action Alliance, mothered by Gloria

Steinem; and Mothers Against Drunk Driving, organized by Candy Lightner.

All these changes in the private nonprofit sphere have paralleled and been reinforced by the greatly increased numbers of women professionals, business executives, and elected or appointed officials at the local, state, and national levels. These trends continue at an accelerating pace.

The feminization of foundation staffs and boards has already been recounted; however, it is in the crucial function of donorship that the multiple roles and growing influence of women are now for the first time becoming understood. Traditionally, men were assumed to be dominant in donorship: almost exclusively they made and controlled the personal fortunes and they created and controlled the foundations they established until they died. Women were not recognized as significant players in the process, despite the considerable number of such exceptional cases as those reviewed in the preceding chapter.

Now however it is being recognized that women, despite their general disenfranchisement and their inferior legal and economic position throughout the eighteenth and nineteenth centuries and well into the twentieth, were in fact influential factors in the evolution of American philanthropy. Little by little, it is being discovered that women for at least two centuries have played an extremely important concomitant and parallel role in philanthropy in many hitherto unrecognized ways.

Again, examples are the clearest way to uncover the reality:

First, women have often been the inspiration and have instilled the values that have led husbands, sons, and families to become active in philanthropy. Ewing M. Kauffman and James E. Casey, major contemporary donors, have eloquently acknowledged this influence. Phoebe Waterman Haas, in the creation of the fine William Penn Foundation in Philadelphia, and Edna McConnell Clark, of the family foundation bearing her name in New York, are just two of many impressive similar examples.

Second, in the formation of the multitude of small and midsize philanthropic funds administered by community foundations, women family members have very often played the key role. The heads of such foundations, which now exist in many cities, can testify to the frequency of this phenomenon.

Third, women have been active partners with their husbands or sons in establishing and shaping joint philanthropic programs. Outstanding examples are Mrs. Steven V. Harkness and her son Edward in the development of the Commonwealth Fund, Lucille Packard and her husband in launching their large foundation, Mabel Beckman and her husband in the evolution of the Beckman Foundation, Adele and Donald Hall in leading the Hall Family Foundation, and Mrs. Sam Walton in launching the huge Walton Foundation.

There are other crucial and unclassifiable instances of the immense influence of certain women on American philanthropy. Most notable was Mrs. Edsel Ford, who survived both her husband and his father, Henry Ford, and who in the early 1950s made the key decisions that saved the Ford Motor Company from disaster. That in turn enabled the inchoate Ford Foundation to get off to a good start. Her good judgment in bringing in new management rescued the floundering automobile company from impending bankruptcy, and the steps she took to assemble a responsible board and define the initial program for the foundation were brilliant.

In the foreseeable future, despite the changes taking place in their status in American life, this important collaborative role of women in philanthropic donorship is unlikely to diminish greatly, and its continuing importance, even its essentiality, should be recognized. The great majority of private fortunes in the United States are still made and controlled by men. Yet in many instances, women, from a presumably subordinate or derivative position, have been primary influences on the development of first-rate foundations established by their husbands, fathers, and in some cases, sons.

All in all, the impact on American philanthropy of women in these collaborative, indirect, and behind-the-scenes roles has been very great and its importance deserves to be recognized.

The pervasive and marked increase in the women's general influence in the field stops short of empowerment in the fullest sense of the term. Yet there are at least three parallel developments now underway or in immediate prospect that may bring women much closer to that status.

The first is the rapid development of the "women's funds." These new foundations trace their origin to the establishment of the Ms. Foundation in 1973, set up with profits from *Ms.* magazine, headed by Gloria Steinem.

There are now more than sixty of these funds in communities across the nation, and their number and their assets have been growing rapidly. Their resources are provided by multiple donors. The feature common to all of them is the intent to fund innovative programs addressing issues facing women and girls that have been neglected by other funding sources.

The fact that women are disproportionately in poverty in the U.S. and suffer a range of special needs and problems—combined with the fact that only a small portion of foundation funds now go to programs for women and girls—sparked the movement, and it is rapidly growing.

The National Network of Women's Funds, the central organization of these foundations, describes its objectives in terms of the following vision: "Imagine a world where women are paid equitably for work, live in homes and communities without fear of physical violence, have chances and choices for themselves and their children, have equal voices in the political process, and serve as the primary decision-makers about issues that affect them. Imagine the justice and opportunities that we all deserve."

This movement is still in its early stages. It is actively at work to expand and stabilize its funding by tapping into payroll deduction plans for women, for example, as well as by seeking contributions from women professionals and those with inherited wealth.

The second development that will strengthen the independent role and influence of women in philanthropy is the growing number of American women who control their own money. These include successful entrepreneurs like Donna Karan and Georgette Klinger as well as women who capably manage their inherited properties and investments, such as Katharine Graham, Oveta Culp Hobby, and Anne Cox Chambers in publishing, Margaret Hunt Hill in oil and real estate, and Lillian Bounds Disney with her diversified business interests. The result is that since 1970 growing numbers of foundations have been set up by women, and overall about one-quarter of new foundations are their creations.

A third development with potentially immense impact on the power of women as independent donors is a small but important change enacted in the United States tax laws in 1986. Called the "unlimited marital deduction," it permits a husband at his death to convey all his wealth to his wife free of any estate taxes. Because of the vast wealth accumulated in recent decades in the United States, several trillions of dollars in inheritances will pass to heirs and descendants in the coming decade or two. Since wives typically out-live their husbands, and because many wealthy men have little or no interest in philanthropy and may leave that matter to their wid-ows, the possible financial implications of this development are enormous.

So it may well be that the important role of women in American philanthropy, long unrecognized, is not only now coming to the fore and increasing at a vigorous rate, but may well take a quantum leap upward in the foreseeable future. If that happens, there are some strong reasons to be hopeful about the consequences. The status of women in American life is generally rising—and so are their competence and confidence in undertaking major new ini-tiatives in many fields. Their past accomplishments should only in-crease the motivation of the coming generations of women donors for high achievement and provide them with valuable role models.

It is also encouraging that many of the most threatening prob-lems of American life today—family breakdown, education, health care, care of the elderly, and racial and sexual discrimination—are precisely the fields in which many American women have concen-trated their charitable efforts in the past. It therefore seems likely that the priorities of the new wave of foundations created and di-rected by women donors will match the nation's most urgent so-cial needs.

Another, somewhat less inspiring, way to try to gauge the future empowerment of women in philanthropy is to look at the records of the various major women donors in recent years. They are mixed. Two of the best have been Lila Acheson Wallace, who with her hus-band, DeWitt Wallace, built the *Reader's Digest* empire, and Lucille Markey, American entrepreneur and famed horse breeder, whose Calumet Farms produced eight Kentucky Derby winners.

Lila Wallace was an extraordinarily generous donor once she became wealthy. Before her death she arranged for her huge fortune to go to a set of premier cultural institutions in the New York City area. Even though control of the Wallace publications has since passed into the hands of an aggressive company executive with a different perspective, her charitable arrangements cannot be diverted.

Lucille Markey, as her wealth began to outstrip her needs in her later years, intelligently went about organizing her philanthropy. She sought good advice in deciding on its field of concentration, namely medical research. She selected high-caliber staff, and she specified that all the funds, in order to have perceptible impact, had to be distributed within fifteen years of her death. Since her death in July 1982 her foundation has built a fine reputation for its effective grantmaking. Her foundation will cease operations June 30, 1997.

Some other cases are more ambiguous. Joan Kroc, widow of the builder of the worldwide McDonald's fast-food chain, has set up her own foundation "to help people accept and overcome conditions that may undermine individual worth and family love." But the program and the focus of her giving are still unclear.

Barbara Piasecka Johnson, a former chambermaid, inherited the fortune of her aged husband, Seward Johnson, under circumstances that led to scandal and bitter litigation with his family. Since those disputes have been resolved, she has built a lavish 160-acre estate in New Jersey, spent $100 million on an art collection, and set up a foundation. The foundation undertook some grandiose (and now failed) efforts to implant capitalistic enterprises in post-Communist Poland, her homeland. But at least she aimed high.

There is nothing surprising, of course, in the fact that some women prove to be far more competent donors than others, since male donors have profusely demonstrated that fact over the decades. The more disturbing question is whether wealthy American women in the future will show as little commitment to philanthropy and charitable giving as the current huge generation of wealthy Americans, men and women, seem to display. This is a matter of very great concern that will be more thoroughly examined in a later chapter.

Part Four

—❧❦❧—

*The Hazards
of Donorship*

Chapter Eight

—◦°₂ᶟᵛᵍ—

Some Cautionary Calamities

Garrison Keillor describes Lake Wobegon, the mythical small town from which his popular radio program supposedly emanates, as a place "where women are strong, men are good-looking, and all the children are above average." That is about the impression one gets of foundations from their annual reports and the routine coverage by the press of their grant announcements. Benign intentions, great competence, and unfailing success in their efforts are the carefully cultivated images.

The reality as regards large foundations is that because of their great resources, they frequently generate deep and powerful conflicts—among members of the donor family, between family members and officers of the donor's company, with public authorities, and sometimes between the donor and the foundation he or she has created. At root these clashes involve both money and power on a large scale, and they are not infrequently intensified by the passions of festering family relationships. A new foundation can be made up of highly fissionable, even explosive elements. The actual cases of conflict and eruption are frequent enough, and often so passionate and destructive that every major new donor should understand this dangerous downside of donorship.

The evidence is that perhaps one-third of new major foundations get into difficulties ranging from bitter internal disputes to long-running major calamities before they become reasonably effective philanthropic institutions. And a few never do.

This is an extraordinarily high accident rate, especially since most new foundations are started by individuals who, almost by definition, have had long and successful experience in the launching and leadership of new enterprises. Clearly, then, building an effective foundation and philanthropic program is a difficult task, with its own special requirements and its special hazards.

Two thought-provoking cases worth analyzing are Alfred I. DuPont's Nemours Foundation and Howard Hughes' huge Medical Institute, which is now the country's largest foundation in assets. Neither donor had a genuine philanthropic intent, but one of these foundations has become a permanent calamity, while the other is an unexpected triumph.

Philanthropy's Oldest Permanent, Established Scandal

Alfred I. DuPont was an able businessman who effectively led the development of his family's great company in the early decades of the twentieth century. But his increasingly bizarre personal behavior and numerous marriages eventually made him a family outcast. His spacious Delaware estate, called Nemours, had a wall around it studded with broken glass "to keep out intruders," as he said, "mainly of the name of DuPont."

In 1932, after a shotgun accident had blinded him in one eye and he had gone deaf, Alfred set up the Nemours Foundation. His plan was carefully contrived so that the foundation could at no point interfere with the management or control of his estate, which was placed in the hands of four trustees "to have and to hold . . . forever."

In time, and after Alfred's death in 1935, Ed Ball, the brother of his last wife, Jessie Ball DuPont, held total control of the trust. By skillful investments he built its corpus to enormous size. (The assets of the foundation are currently on the order of $500 million, and those of the trust are estimated to be some $1.8 billion.)

The philanthropic activities of the foundation have never been more than inconsequential and at times have even been fraudulent. Its primary purpose has been the maintenance of the gardens and mansion of the donor's Delaware estate as a public park. The secondary purpose has been the support of a hospital facility for the care and treatment of crippled children.

Early on, the performance of the hospital became so inadequate that the attorney general of Delaware at one point sued the foundation for failure to fulfill its charitable obligations and imposed a multimillion-dollar fine. Subsequently the attorneys general of both Delaware and Florida charged the trust with hoarding income at the expense of the Nemours Foundation's charities.

As of October 1994 the trust and the foundation were still in the headlines. The major properties of the trust were assembled by Ed Ball before his death in 1967, most of them located in Florida. But the trust is now stagnating, minority shareholders in some of the companies and banks it controls are protesting, and a reorganization may be pending. Meanwhile—as a philanthropy—the Nemours Foundation remains a gigantic and long-standing disgrace.

The Most Unlikely Transformation

The Howard Hughes Medical Institute, technically classified as an operating foundation, is the largest in the country, with an endowment of more than $8 billion. For some twenty years after its creation it remained an utterly nonfunctioning foundation with no purpose other than serving as a tax-avoidance device for its donor.

Howard Hughes, the donor, was one of the century's most gifted and most bizarre business entrepreneurs. He inherited a small and profitable manufacturing company from his father; and building on that base, he became a billionaire defense contractor, movie tycoon, and airline operator. A pilot himself, he once held the transcontinental speed record. But he became more famous as the consort of movie queens and as a Las Vegas playboy.

Always a neurotic and erratic personality, Hughes became increasingly paranoid and reclusive in his later years, obsessed with secrecy and with keeping himself germ-free. He spent his last years sitting alone, naked and long-haired, in his darkened hotel hideaway watching B movies. A drug addict, he died of kidney disease in 1976.

Hughes' major philanthropic creation was purely inadvertent. With no interest in medicine or philanthropy, he set up his medical institute in 1953 as a tax shield for his aircraft manufacturing company. In 1955 the Internal Revenue Service denied special tax-exempt status for it on the grounds that it "was merely siphoning off taxable income into an exempt foundation." But a year later Hughes arranged a $205,000 loan to then Vice President Nixon's brother, and three months later the IRS, improbably by coincidence, reversed that ruling.

For the next twenty years the institute limped along with Hughes himself as the sole trustee and with little income, most of it fed back into the aircraft company for rent and other charges. In that entire period Hughes had no communication whatever with the "director" either by letter, telephone, or in person.

Hughes died in 1976, and his will was in litigation for the next seven years. In 1983 the attorney general of Delaware won a court suit to force the institute to enlarge its board of trustees and to permit him to name half of the new members. He subsequently appointed a group of individuals of high standing to the new places on the board.

From that moment the foundation became a much different and better operation. Its budget rose from $15 million a year at the time of Hughes' death to more than $300 million a year by the mid-1990s. It now concentrates its work on research in the basic sciences, principally in the field of medicine, and on medical education. It has established laboratories at more than fifty leading academic medical centers, hospitals, and universities throughout the country, where it supports some 2,100 pre- and postdoctoral scientists.

Although the Hughes Medical Institute has since had some small and embarrassing mishaps in its development, it now has an eminent and effective board and a staff of outstanding medical authorities. It has become one of the world's largest and most important centers of research and training in the health field. No more magnificent phoenix has ever risen from such an unpromising pile of ashes in the history of philanthropy.

If there are lessons to be learned from these two contrasting cases for the upcoming wave of American donors, they may be, first, that a selfish and unphilanthropic donor like Alfred DuPont is very likely to produce a corrupt and ineffective foundation. And second, that the American philanthropic ethos and tradition are so strong that the foundation of even a bizarre and mindless donor like Howard Hughes can sometimes be rescued by a combination of alert government overseers and some public-spirited citizen trustees.

Two Paradoxes:
Dedicated Donors, Disastrous Outcomes

The Land Foundation of Massachusetts was established after World War II by a scientific genius, Edwin Land, from whose laboratories had come a succession of important research achievements in polarized light, photography, and color television. On the basis of these discoveries Land created the Polaroid company, which in the 1960s was one of the most rapidly growing and profitable corporations in the United States.

During this period Land began using both his company and the foundation he had established to advance various social and educational reforms in which he ardently believed. He attempted to use his company as an instrument of social change "to arrive at a one-class society." As he once told his employees, he wanted to help build "a society in which there is no hierarchy.... We have brought into industry from feudal times a feudal structure. . . . What we would like to build at Polaroid is a nonfeudal society."

Under Land's leadership the company also took vigorous steps to give employment opportunities to blacks and to give every employee the chance to do research in addition to his or her routine duties. Land also made major grants to Harvard and the Massachusetts Institute of Technology to introduce new approaches to teaching young scientists, and he set up a special trust fund to provide research opportunities for exceptionally talented undergraduates.

At the time it seemed that the buoyant force of a great new donor had appeared and that Land's impact would be felt on problems as diverse as those of human development, scientific advancement, and the enrichment of the industrial work environment.

This creative, evangelistic, and reform-minded philanthropist was at the same time the dominating head of his company, about whose future he was fervently optimistic. As a result, he kept all the assets of his foundation in Polaroid stock—which in his view maximized the prospects for the foundation's future growth. But that proved to be its undoing.

In the mid-1970s the company bet its future on a revolutionary new instant camera called the X–120. The product proved to be a disastrous failure, and the price of Polaroid shares collapsed. Within a short time Land was removed from his executive role in the company, and his foundation ultimately had to be closed down. His risky investment policy had extinguished what had been seen as a bright new hope for American philanthropy.

Harry John's DeRance Foundation of Wisconsin offers another, and more bizarre, example of a generous and dedicated donor who rather late in life destroyed his control of his own foundation by mishandling its investments.

John was the somewhat eccentric heir to half the Miller Brewing Company fortune. A fervent Catholic, he took the proceeds of his inheritance—some $100 million—and put virtually all of it into his foundation, named after a sixteenth-century Roman Catholic monk.

For the next thirty years John, his wife, Erica, and his religious advisor, Donald Gallagher, traveled the world visiting leprosaria, orphanages, remote rural hospitals, and similar Catholic institutions. The multitude of grants given by the DeRance Foundation in that long period reflected great compassion and concern for people of every color who were in desperate need. No other large American foundation so concentrated its efforts on such individuals. John himself worked tirelessly on foundation matters, and he and his wife and their several children lived in the most modest style in a little house in Milwaukee, Wisconsin.

Then in the mid-1970s John decided to shift the foundation's focus to the United States and to the education of Catholics in religious matters via television. He thereupon acquired a small chain of stations and invested several million dollars of the foundation's funds in building and equipping a modern television production studio to supply programs to those stations.

But he planned that his new Catholic network would be under his personal control, not that of the church hierarchy. That, according to one plausible view, may have led to his eventual downfall.

It appears that the danger and possible divisiveness of such an independent Catholic network at a time of growing conflict on various doctrinal and moral issues within the church then became of serious concern to the Vatican. Its representative in Washington at the time, a Monsignor Longhi, summoned Mrs. John and Donald Gallagher (they, plus Mr. John, made up the foundation's board) and reportedly told them they had two choices: file a lawsuit to remove Mr. John from his controlling position in the foundation and abort the plans for the television network, or face excommunication.

The direct hand of the Vatican in the matter has never been proved, but in fact such a suit was placed by Mrs. John shortly after the conversations with Monsignor Longhi. It initially charged John with "improper and profligate spending" on his television project.

In the course of the discovery process by the plaintiff's lawyers, evidence was found of improper actions in John's handling of the foundation's investments. On the basis of those findings, the charges against him were modified, and he was convicted by the court of violating his fiduciary responsibilities as a trustee. For this he was not simply fined or sentenced to a jail term; instead, he was ordered removed from any contact with and any authority over his own foundation.

Immediately thereafter, indeed almost instantly, a senior executive of a major American corporation headed by a leading Catholic layman was rushed into the situation to liquidate the television project as quickly as possible.

John subsequently appealed his ouster, but without success. Thereafter the DeRance Foundation, under the direction of the now-divorced Mrs. John, continued quietly, almost invisibly, to distribute small charitable gifts to various Catholic charities, leaving the cloud of mystery surrounding the case intact and impenetrable until 1992 when the whole story came to a bizarre, even grotesque end. Harry John, living alone and in seclusion in California, had been informed by his lawyers that although he was excluded from participating in the activities of the DeRance Foundation, he had the legal right to determine the disposition of its remaining assets at the time of his death. Accordingly, he created the shell of a new foundation, called Southern Cross, outlined its projected program, named several individuals to its board, and specified in his will that it was to receive all of the remaining assets of the DeRance Foundation after his death. Those assets remained at a level of some $100 million.

Late in that year he suffered a massive stroke and heart attack. At a certain moment his doctor declared him essentially vegetative and declined to prescribe any further drastic life-sustaining measures. Almost immediately his former wife appeared on the scene and ordered that such measures be taken, and as a result some minimal signs of life continued for an additional two days. In that brief period the tiny "board" of the DeRance Foundation disposed of all its remaining assets—there was a $70 million grant to the Archdiocese of Milwaukee, and the remainder went in a group of smaller $1 million–plus grants to several other Catholic charities.

Thus, at the moment of Harry John's final expiration, there were no remaining assets in the DeRance Foundation, and his final plans were foiled. So ended one of the most bizarre examples in philanthropy of the frustration of a donor's intentions. An ascetic by nature, Harry John had brought on himself and his foundation these disasters by his own peculiar impulse for financial finagling. Nonetheless, his punishment did not quite seem to fit the crime.

If some moral can be drawn from these two very different instances, it may be that the launching of a large foundation is inherently risky, and it becomes especially so under the domination of a fervent and strong-minded donor. Land, potentially a great donor, was disastrously imprudent in the handling of the investments of his foundation. John, a man of long dedication to charitable works, was either recklessly irresponsible in seeking some small personal gain from his handling of his foundation's investments, or he was recklessly imprudent in thinking he could challenge the power of the hierarchy of his church, or both.

In any event, the Land and DeRance cases are vivid reminders that benign institutions like foundations are not exempt from the hazards and unforeseen misfortunes that beset every other kind of human enterprise. They also illustrate that the situations that arise in foundation building are so diverse, complex, and sometimes unexpected that no simple rules for success can be laid down, nor can predictions be made as to outcomes.

Chapter Nine

—⁂—

Some Near Calamities and Great Escapes

The list of the major calamities recounted in the preceding chapter is sobering, but in some ways it is even more instructive to examine the near calamities and the hairbreadth escapes from impending disaster that some foundations have managed to accomplish. These cases have been very different from one another, but they all suggest that even in the most corrupt or contentious situations, well-intentioned and courageous individuals can sometimes be motivated to intervene and try to salvage the situation. And in some cases, including some very major ones, they can succeed.

Indeed, even when appalling mistakes have been made—by donors or by trustees or staff—things can sometimes still be made to turn out reasonably well. The following examples differ greatly from one another, but they all are instructive.

Hartford Foundation

The Hartford Foundation was created in 1929 by the brothers who had developed their A&P grocery stores in the early decades of the century into the first national supermarket chain. The foundation was set up mainly as a device to prevent any takeover of the company by outside interests, but by the late 1950s, after the brothers had died, both the foundation and the company were stagnant and in decline under the control of a group of old company executives plus a few family members. The foundation's somewhat amateurish and inconsequential program in the medical field caused no internal strains, but with the drop in company profits the relatives of the donors became more and more agitated because of the corresponding decrease in the value of their share holdings. A protracted struggle between the two groups then developed. This continued through the 1960s with no prospect of a resolution.

However, in the late 1960s when Congressman Wright Patman launched a series of attacks on foundations, including criticism of the Hartford Foundation specifically, Hartford's old guard was impelled to reach beyond the ranks of former A&P executives to find an independent trustee. They did not reach out very far, however, selecting Leonard Dalsemer, a friend from Lyford Key, then a favorite winter resort of A&P retirees. He turned out to be an unexpectedly vigorous and able housecleaner.

In his business career Dalsemer had been a successful publisher and private investor. With a hard-driving, entrepreneurial style, he quickly took charge. In response to legislation in 1969 prohibiting "excess business holdings" by foundations, he found a German buyer for a large block of the foundation's A&P holdings and engineered the board's acceptance of the deal. Once that crucial step was accomplished, the new trustee proceeded to rehabilitate the foundation's program, bringing in a first-rate director from another foundation. He also instituted a proper endowment-management system. By 1980, ten years after he had come aboard, the Hartford Foundation was a modernized and invigorated institution—due in large degree to the selfless dedication and vision of this one man.

The sequel to the story, however, contained another unanticipated twist. For some reasons that are as mystifying as his earlier zeal in modernizing and invigorating the Hartford Foundation, Dalsemer later became such a dictatorial and oppressive force in the institution that his death and departure a few years later were generally welcomed by the able people in the fine foundation that he had done so much to build.

The good work of the Hartford Foundation continues. Its current emphasis is on the unique health needs of the elderly and the problem of maintaining the quality of medical care while controlling its costs.

Weingart Foundation

The Weingart Foundation of California was created by a donor who, starting with virtually nothing, had built a considerable fortune in real estate in the early boom years in Los Angeles. At his death he simply abandoned his fortune to the shell of his foundation. A bachelor, he was quoted during the last days of his life as saying, "If I could, I'd just order a bigger shroud and take my money with me." He had, however, named three business acquaintances as trustees. They were not close friends of his, but at his request they agreed to serve. His only guidance to them was his interest, growing out of his own miserably poor early years, in the problems of the down-and-out.

After his death the little group of trustees had to construct the foundation from the ground up. Furthermore, they faced the unexpected burden of long and disagreeable litigation brought by one of Weingart's several paramours, who was determined to break his will. Approaching the challenge with patience and dedication, they saw the foundation through lengthy litigation. Eventually a settlement permitted them to give attention to the development of a program, the hiring of a staff, and the management of the foundation's assets, which included extensive real-estate holdings.

To discover and reconstruct Weingart's intentions, the trustees investigated his history and learned that he had lived with foster parents as a boy, been a field hand in Georgia, and eventually worked delivering laundry along Los Angeles's skid row. One clue to his intentions was a statement he had once made that he had met some very nice people on skid row: "As nice as you would meet anywhere. An awful lot of them just had bad luck or were simply old and unwanted. I remembered them the rest of my life."

With this as their lodestone, the trustees began by developing a program with an unusual emphasis on serving the needs of the down-and-out. That effort continues, but with the growth of the foundation's assets, which are now on the order of $600 million, its program has broadened to include a range of efforts in behalf of children and youth in low-income neighborhoods in the six southern counties of California.

The Weingart Foundation's board and staff are exceptionally strong; and with them, the present scale of its resources, and the clear priorities of its program, it has the potential to be a powerful force for social change in the area. The story of the rescue of this orphan foundation has already had a very happy ending.

Aaron Diamond Foundation

The Aaron Diamond Foundation is a stark case of snatching philanthropic victory from the jaws of death—a drama in which by sheer chance a new, large foundation was saved from corruption and calamity.

The donor was a successful New York City real-estate operator whose business ethics were shadowed and who surrounded himself with associates most of whom were in frequent difficulty with the law. His wife, Irene, a former actor and film executive, had a serious interest in various cultural activities and public-affairs issues, but she had no business experience whatever.

Almost immediately after Diamond's death two of his principal advisors, who were handling his estate, presented his wife with a substantial bundle of legal papers which, she was told, she had to sign immediately. It has to be assumed that they believed she would comply simply because of her innocence in such matters and because of the forbidding complexity of the documents. However, Irene Diamond sought outside advice.

It happened that she was well acquainted with Wilbur H. Ferry, a man of wide practical experience and also knowledgeable about philanthropy. Ferry had served as an advisor to Henry Ford II in the early years of the Ford Foundation and later as an associate director of the Fund for the Republic, the civil liberties project headed by Robert M. Hutchins, former head of the University of Chicago.

Ferry, at Irene Diamond's request, suggested a young man, Vincent McGee, to help her organize the new foundation set up in her husband's will. McGee happened to be with her at the moment the fateful bundle of papers arrived to be signed. At her request he read through them. Although he was not a lawyer, he quickly realized they constituted a total conveyance of control over her husband's property, including the assets of the foundation, to the two principal advisors—a bold and brazen attempt at appropriation by these two men.

Irene Diamond immediately employed independent counsel, and what followed was fast and ugly. Brutal threats were made, but she stood fast, and in the end the takeover effort was frustrated.

The building of the foundation then began, and it quickly took an interesting form. Mrs. Diamond had clear objectives in mind: medical research, minority education, and cultural programs, all in New York City. To make sure the foundation had impact on these objectives, she decided that all its resources should be expended within ten years.

Mrs. Diamond and McGee, who had been a vigorous civil rights activist and had served a prison term as a Vietnam War protester, have been able to work compatibly with each other. Together these two strong-minded individuals have built an outstanding board of trustees and a vigorous program that is focused on minority education, cultural projects, AIDS research, and civil and human rights.

Grantees praise the Diamond Foundation as one of the few that regularly gives people general-support grants. It is prepared to trust the judgment of people who know what they want to do and how to do it.

The foundation has only until 1997 to spend the balance of its funds. When it is gone, it will be greatly missed.

The Hartford, Weingart, and Diamond cases are three of the more important near calamities and recoveries among midsize foundations in the last half-century. Factors ranging from chance to pure and powerful motivation, to public service on the part of family members and even strangers, have operated to salvage these situations. Their outcomes could otherwise have been at best dismal and at worst disgraceful, even dangerous, in terms of the public interest.

There are three other examples of very large foundations that might well have become disasters but, in defiance of the odds, did not. They are the Robert Wood Johnson Foundation, whose assets of $3.6 billion make it the sixth largest in the country; the MacArthur Foundation, the fourth biggest, with assets of $3.7 billion; and the Ford Foundation, the largest, with assets of $6.5 billion.

Robert Wood Johnson Foundation

The Robert Wood Johnson Foundation of New Jersey was established by a most able and successful businessman who headed his family's pharmaceutical company during its period of greatest growth. Robert Wood Johnson was also a man with wide interests in science and social policy, and he was active in political and public affairs throughout his life. His interest in philanthropy began early. He set up his foundation in 1936, thirty years before his death, and used it to support various projects that interested him, such as the creation of the nation's first school of hospital administration at Northwestern University. Later hoping to avoid the kinds of family quarrels that have troubled other large foundations, he carefully set up a small separate foundation through which his family could give to their particular charitable interests.

Despite such wisdom and foresight, Johnson did things that were likely to breed future problems. He wanted his foundation to work on problems of health care, the same field in which his company was involved, a combination which might well have led to troublesome conflicts of interest. Equally questionable, and for the same reason, was the control that he gave over his foundation to a group of Johnson and Johnson company executives that he made its trustees. To head the board, he designated Gustav O. Lienhard, who was president of his company. Besides those chancy steps, he made no effort to structure or activate his foundation while he was alive so that he could steer it back if it got off course.

The experience of the Lilly Foundation, in a comparable relationship to the donor's pharmaceutical company, could have alerted Johnson to the possible dangers of such arrangements: it was plagued with conflicts of interest for many years and burdened with overage company executives put out to pasture by placing them on the foundation's board.

Johnson died in 1968, and almost immediately things began to happen—good things, not bad ones. All the trustees soon separated themselves from the company. Lienhard, immediately after his retirement, plunged into an intensive study of the field of philanthropy, consulting knowledgeable people throughout the country. He was determined that the foundation should become not only a good one but a leader in its field. He then took nearly a year scouring the country for the right man to become the new president. He found him in David Rogers, then head of the prestigious medical school of Johns Hopkins University.

So a basically conservative board of men with strong ties to the medical establishment were joined with an educator and physician who was an activist reformer in creating new kinds of systems for the delivery of health services. It seemed unlikely that such a combination could work together harmoniously.

An additional potential problem was that Lienhard insisted on operating as a full-time chairman with an office adjacent to that of the president, so Rogers had to try to run the foundation with a mother-in-law constantly in his kitchen. Nevertheless, and in defiance of the odds, things worked out spectacularly.

Over the following decade the Robert Wood Johnson Foundation compiled a brilliant record. With the extraordinarily talented staff that Rogers assembled, it carried out some thirty major field trials of new approaches to health care—for the handicapped, for rural communities, for school children, for the aged, and others—all of national scope and with carefully planned scientific evaluations of their results.

However, during the second decade after Johnson's death things began to come apart. Lienhard became more dictatorial, and Rogers, finally fed up, left. Some of his best staff followed. Since then, the board has become more diversified, a new generation of able staff has been recruited, and though it has not quite regained its earlier brilliance, the foundation remains a very fine institution.

Yet, with the chances the donor took in involving his old company officers so heavily in the foundation during its formative period, things could well have turned out very badly.

Ford Foundation

The Ford Foundation stands as the most monumental disaster in American philanthropy that didn't happen. It was created on paper in the 1930s by Edsel Ford and his wife, Eleanor Clay Ford, both of whom had some interest in philanthropy, and with the acquiescence of Edsel's father, automaker Henry Ford, who had almost none. The original intent was simply to create a vehicle to distribute gifts to various local charities.

By 1948 both Edsel and his father had died, and the foundation had inherited ownership of nearly all the shares of the motor company. Edsel's son, Henry Ford II, had left college to take over as head of the huge and very troubled family firm. It was suffering deadly losses, and a gang of thugs under Harry Bennett, former bodyguard of the old man, were still on the premises and virtually in control.

There were many days when young Henry had to carry a pistol to the office as he went about his task of cleaning up the managerial mess of the dying company he had inherited.

It was in that same period he learned—without joy—that he had also inherited the chairmanship of the board of the Ford Foundation along with his many other responsibilities. As he said to a close advisor, when handed the docket for the first trustees meeting he attended: "This stuff just isn't my line of country. What I want to do is build automobiles."

But things began to improve on the business front. The Bennett gang was ousted, an able executive was hired to overhaul the company, and within two years profits were beginning to roll in. In turn, the foundation's income grew. If the company continued to prosper, it was clear that the foundation was destined to become very large, quite possibly the largest in the country. A decision was therefore made—probably at the urging of Edsel's widow, Eleanor, who was the wise and strong character in the whole drama—to create a committee of experts to examine what the structure and the program of the foundation should be. It is also likely that Eleanor was advised to do this by Dr. Karl Compton, then head of the Massachusetts Institute of Technology and a director of the motor company.

A bright young lawyer, Rowan Gaither, who had worked with Dr. Compton on a major scientific project during World War II, was chosen to head the committee of experts. He selected a diverse and talented group to work with him, one of whom, William Mc-Peak, formerly with the American Heart Association, turned out to be a creative genius in the design of the massive new entity.

The committee worked for two years, consulting with individuals and groups throughout the country. Their Study Report still stands as the finest effort of its kind to set a new foundation's priorities and define its role on a rational and carefully studied basis. In 1952, with this document as its guide, the board hired the Ford Foundation's first president, Paul Hoffman, a former businessman who had gained worldwide prestige as head of the just-completed Marshall Plan. Hoffman in turn brought in a high-powered group of senior program directors—possibly too high-powered for the tame world of philanthropy. This team, which included Robert Maynard Hutchins (the brilliant and controversial former head of the University of Chicago), promptly launched a series of dramatic new ventures, both domestic and international. Their actions won great acclaim.

Thereafter, however, some serious problems developed. Hoffman became so engaged in the 1953 Eisenhower presidential campaign that he neglected the foundation and was deposed at the end of that year. It also happened that McCarthyism was on the rise at that time as the Cold War era set in. Hutchins, an ardent and extremely controversial defender of civil liberties, became a lightning rod that attracted relentless right-wing attacks on the foundation because of his association with it. As a result, for the next few years the foundation's energies were drained by a series of congressional investigations and sustained media campaigns against it.

But the foundation weathered the storm and survived. Under a succession of presidents, some low-key and others high-profile, it has had its ups and downs, yet on the whole it has been infinitely better than what might have been. Much credit must be given to those unsung heroes—including Eleanor Clay Ford, Rowan Gaither, William McPeak, Henry Ford II, and arguably Robert Hutchins.

These people filled the vacuum left by Henry Ford and his son Edsel and set the foundation on the road to becoming a useful and now generally respected institution, nationally and internationally.

MacArthur Foundation

The MacArthur Foundation of Chicago is the newest and the most riotous example of a near calamity and eventual recovery among foundations.

The donor, John D. MacArthur, was the sleazy and avaricious owner of a large and highly profitable insurance company. Of charitable and civic interests he had none. His relationship with his only son was one of active animosity. He set up his foundation in 1970 for the usual tax avoidance reasons. In the typical pattern of indifferent donors, he stacked its board with old business cronies, plus his wife (who thought the whole idea of a foundation was nonsense and never attended a board meeting). Then, incomprehensibly, he added his son, Rod, with whom he had a terrible relationship, to complete the mélange.

When some of the trustees asked him just before his death in 1978 what he wanted the foundation to do, he clearly had not the vaguest idea. His reply was, "I made the money. You guys will have to figure out what to do with it." With that kind of guidance, the foundation got off to a predictably troubled start. The trustees, who were at the same time mostly officers of the insurance company, faced a situation of inherent and serious conflicts of interest. But at least they shared a faith in the donor's style of rugged individualism. Rod MacArthur, who was himself a self-made and successful entrepreneur, was at the opposite end of the political spectrum from his father, believing that foundations should be "at the cutting edge of social change."

Rod threw himself into the foundation's affairs literally with a vengeance. He had two goals: to clean out what he regarded as a filthy stable and to allocate a large portion of the foundation's funds to support substantial cash awards for "maverick geniuses" around the world. During the first year he also pressed to expand the board by adding some strong, independent trustees, and he urged the diversification of the foundation's controlling holdings in the insurance company.

He lost nearly every battle in the board room. Yet, sensing the vulnerability of the others to charges of conflicts of interest and their fear of publicity about the internal brawling going on, he bludgeoned them with threats of lawsuits, with denunciations in the press conferences he called, and with the careful collection of all kinds of internal records of accounts.

The public had never seen such a spectacle of philanthropic civil war. In the end Rod prevailed. He gained funding for his maverick geniuses project (now called the MacArthur Prize Fellows Program), which has become the foundation's signature achievement. He also won the assent of the other trustees to enlarge the board by seven members. His nominees were individuals of the highest standing, including two world-famous scientists and three former university presidents. Only one, William Simon, former secretary of the treasury under President Nixon, shared the archconservatism of the company-connected trustees—and he resigned in a huff after several months when his proposal to remove Rod from the board was voted down.

This was a watershed, and thereafter the foundation moved generally toward a higher level of performance. But Rod was still not appeased. He repeatedly and publicly charged some board members with mishandling the foundation's assets and taking exorbitant fees, and he accused the company-connected directors with mismanaging the business. In early 1984 he placed a suit containing a catalog of allegations against all but two of the other trustees and asking that the court put the foundation into receivership or dismantle it. The suit never came to a conclusion because during the lengthy proceedings Rod was stricken with cancer and died. Thus ended the strange career of this turbulent factor in the evolution of the MacArthur Foundation.

Rod MacArthur was idealistic, relentless, and tough as an alley cat. He was more than just difficult to deal with; some of his friends, as well as his enemies, felt he was half crazy. But from the standpoint of the public interest, he was on the right side of most of the issues he raised, and he was the only member of the original board to enunciate a concept of the foundation's role commensurate with its huge resources. His methods were rough, but the crucial measure of his success is that after his death the trends toward improvement in the foundation's staff, board, and programs continued.

The answer to the question of why Rod dedicated himself so totally and unrestrainedly to the salvation and transformation of his father's memorial would have to be sought in the deepest reaches of a rejected and detested son's psyche. But had he not forcefully lifted the foundation from where his father left it, it would today quite possibly be a national disgrace. (It is to be noted that Rod, in his own life and apart from his father's foundation, was a successful independent business entrepreneur. Before his death he established his own foundation with his own wealth, the J. Roderick MacArthur Foundation. It carries on a program dedicated to aiding "those who are inequitably or unjustly treated by established institutions.")

Chapter Ten

—⚜—

Contrasting Cases
in the Arts
Lee Krasner and Andy Warhol

The great rise in interest in modern art in the United States in recent decades—and in art prices—has produced a number of artists
of considerable wealth and has already resulted in two substantial
foundations based on such wealth. One is the Pollock-Krasner
Foundation, created by the widow of painter Jackson Pollock, a
major figure in modern American art. The other is the Andy
Warhol Foundation, established in 1987 by another prominent figure in the visual arts.

The Pollock-Krasner Foundation is a remarkable example of
wisdom and integrity in the creation of an outstandingly effective
foundation in the service of artists. The Warhol Foundation, in
contrast, is a troubling ongoing spectacle of greed, conflict, and
disorder. If not brought under control, it could discourage other

wealthy American artists from bequeathing their works to a new foundation.

Pollock–Krasner Foundation

By the time he died in an automobile accident in 1956, Jackson Pollock had become one of the greatest figures in twentieth-century painting. His wife, Lee Krasner, was also a recognized painter. Her talents were obscured by the notoriety of her husband and by her desire not to appear to be in competition with him. But after his death she too gained international stature as an artist.

At the time of their marriage he was penniless and she worked as a waitress in a Greenwich Village restaurant in New York City. As artists they had a long economic struggle that they escaped only in the last few years of his life.

Krasner was a tough-minded and stubborn woman who brooked nonsense from no one. In her later years one writer described her as a "fierce, undeluded woman" with the look of "a beanbag in repose."

She needed to be tough to survive her marriage with Pollock and his alcoholic and psychotic rages. She also needed that same quality to survive the sexism that prevailed in the art world during most of the years she worked in it. For example, her teacher, the famous artist Hans Hofmann, said of one of her paintings in 1937, "This is so good you would not know it was done by a woman."

For all their difficulties, Krasner and Pollock were resolute in their commitment to artistic integrity; and she was equally resolute, despite their endless marital problems, in her faith in Pollock's genius. In the early 1980s, long after his death and when Krasner's own health had begun to fail, her wealth totaled some $20 million, mainly in the form of an inventory of her and Pollock's paintings. Since the couple had been childless, she decided to put it all into a foundation. She stipulated that none of the funds could be used to promote her or Pollock's art, that her husband's name should come first in the foundation's name, and that all the money should be used to help "worthy and needy visual artists" of any age and anywhere in the world.

The Pollock–Krasner foundation came into existence in 1984. Since then it has become a model of intelligent, caring, unbureaucratic philanthropy. It generously and flexibly gives help of almost any kind to alleviate problems of the individual artist—to pay for studio rent, emergency medical care, psychiatric help, or other personal or professional needs. There is no ceiling on the size of grants; they are tailored to each individual circumstance. The application procedure is simple and requests can be submitted at any time of the year. Moreover, grant decisions are made promptly, an almost lost art in foundations generally.

A committee of distinguished persons from the art world judges the applicant's artistic merit ("recognizable though not necessarily recognized excellence," as one has put it). The staff investigates the authenticity of the need, and with that information the trustees decide the allocation of grants. The names of grantees are published only with the permission of the artists, since some (particularly older artists) are reluctant to have their peers know they have received a grant where need is one of the determining factors.

Perhaps most unusual of all, the foundation does not require obsequiousness nor even cordiality on the part of its applicants. In the words of the chief executive officer, "the deference commonly shown to grant makers doesn't exist among artists. We've made grants to antagonistic, even abusive people that other foundations would have thrown out of the office."

By the early 1990s and before the end of its first decade of operation, the Pollock-Krasner Foundation had made nearly a thousand individual grants totaling some $10 million. The responses have been extraordinary: artists have credited their grants with rescuing them from everything from creative blocks to suicide. Each grant has helped its recipient through a particularly difficult crisis—medical, psychological, professional, or financial.

In a quiet way the impact of this foundation's work has penetrated widely in the world of artists. It has accomplished this by its discriminating judgments and a style that is regarded as warmhearted and understanding of the artist's feelings and point of view.

How did that happen? How did Lee Krasner, a woman with no experience whatever in creating organizations, do it? And how, in the sometimes junglelike world of art, art dealers, and chicanery, has this foundation behaved with singular honor, integrity, and sensitivity long after the donor's disappearance?

The answers are instructive.

First, Krasner knew clearly what she wanted her foundation to do, based on her own direct experience as an artist. She understood deeply and personally the struggles and problems of the artist in contemporary America. In a conversation with an old friend shortly before her death, she discussed the kind of worthy causes that she wanted her foundation to serve: "I am an artist. I want it to go to help artists. That's what I know. That's my world."

Second, among Krasner's trusted friends were two individuals of great experience and practical wisdom, and she had the good sense to turn to them for advice. One was Gerald Dickler, a distinguished lawyer who had been her longtime counselor on legal and other matters. The other was Eugene Victor Thaw, one of the most respected and successful private art dealers in the world. Since the creation of the foundation, both have given it their dedicated service as trustees. Thaw has directed the strategy for marketing of the art works that are the foundation's principal asset. He has also coauthored a four-volume *catalogue raisonné* of all Pollock's works.

Third, Krasner was able to convey to Thaw and Dickler not only her intentions regarding the focus of the foundation's efforts but also the style and the feeling that she wanted its operations to reflect. In choosing its administrative head, therefore, they turned to Charles Bergman, who brought to the job a background in the arts, foundation management, and mental health.

So Krasner chose wisely and well in designating her "trustees." An individual of sound judgment and integrity, she recognized those qualities in others, and she built her foundation on such criteria. Because of her own character and wisdom, it has remained remarkably faithful to her intentions.

Andy Warhol Foundation

The Andy Warhol Foundation, created by another well-known American artist, is a far more problematic situation.

Warhol died in 1987. His will left all his assets to the foundation that he had created "for the advancement of the visual arts." These assets included not only his own works but also valuable real estate, a vast collection of antiques and objets d'art, and his own huge collection of contemporary art, which included some seven hundred paintings by other American artists, nine thousand drawings, nineteen thousand prints, and some sixty thousand photographs. Estimates of the value of this bonanza range from $100 million to $800 million.

Because of its holdings, the Warhol Foundation is easily among the two hundred largest American foundations, and depending on whose estimates of its holdings are accepted, it may rank among the top fifty.

Warhol was a very different kind of person from Lee Krasner. In addition to whatever qualities he may have had as an artist, he was a masterful merchandiser of himself and his works, a massive collector and trader of every form of art, a skilled and indefatigable manipulator of the media, and a denizen of some of the sleazier provinces of the art world.

His vision for the foundation he created was vague, however, and the individuals to whom he bequeathed responsibility for it have proved to be a quarrelsome and self-seeking group. In its first few years the foundation, under a succession of heads, has run down its cash, run up its expenses, and generally operated in an uproar. Expenses became considerable partly due to lavish directors' fees and a brutal legal dispute with the former lawyer for the estate. In this initial period the foundation began to make some grants, but a good portion of them went to favorite charities of the board members.

When critics of the foundation, including those on the inside, have raised questions about the chaos of its program, the foundation's response has been that it would be a disservice to hold the legacy of an artist as unpredictable as Andy Warhol to a regimen. In the words of the foundation's program director, "To have made a strict mission would not have been terribly Warholian."

By 1994 the new director, Archibald Gillies, was calling his role "a rescue mission" and he launched a $125,000 public relations blitz to embellish the foundation's deteriorating image. But the volatile mixture of egos and conflicting individual interests was producing a fusillade of public charges by the leading figures involved of mismanagement, of claims for exorbitant fees, and of misappropriation of funds.

There are some serious people involved in the foundation who are trying to dig it out of the debris of its initial calamities, but its prospects after a very troubled first few years are still quite unclear. As it grapples with its problems, more is at stake than the survival of a single foundation, or how an important modern artist will be remembered. As the *New York Times* commented on the situation in June 1994, the fate of the Warhol Foundation "could help determine whether other contemporary artists like Roy Lichtenstein and Jasper Johns will feel comfortable leaving their own considerable fortunes to philanthropy."

Such wealthy artists and potential donors can, however, lift their comfort level by reflecting on the wisdom shown by Lee Krasner in selecting the individuals to whom she entrusted the leadership of her foundation. And by reflecting also on the values, vagaries, and mindlessness of Andy Warhol in launching his.

Walter H. Annenberg *(UPI/Bettmann)*

Edward S. and Anna Harkness
(UPI/Bettmann)

James Buchanan Duke
(UPI/Bettmann)

Edsel and Eleanor Clay Ford *(UPI/Bettmann)*

Lee Krasner *(Photo by Ann Chwatsky, courtesy The Pollock-Krasner Foundation)*

Andrew Carnegie
aboard ship
(UPI/Bettmann)

Lucile P. Markey *(Photo
© Ray Fisher)*

Lloyd Noble *(University of Oklahoma)*

Julius Rosenwald
(UPI/Bettmann)

David Packard and President Ronald Reagan *(UPI/Bettmann)*

John D. Rockefeller Sr. has his golf club chalked by a caddy (1931). *(UPI/Bettmann)*

Jim and Patty Rouse *(Photo by Janis Rettallata, courtesy The Enterprise Foundation)*

Olivia Slocum Sage
(UPI/Bettmann)

Ellen Scripps
(UPI/Bettmann)

Gloria Steinem *(UPI/Bettmann)*

Boris Yeltsin and George Soros
(UPI/Bettmann)

Lila Acheson Wallace
(UPI/Bettmann)

John Olin *(Sports Illustrated)*

Part Five

—ৡৢৣৢৡ—

*The Great
Middle Kingdom*

—⸎—

Family Foundations, Family Problems

By definition family foundations are created by the head of a family and subsequently remain under the control of his or her descendants and their spouses. They make up the great Middle Kingdom of American philanthropy: probably three-quarters of the nearly 35,000 private foundations in the United States are of this type.

Most are quite small: about 90 percent have assets of less than $1 million; another 5 to 10 percent have assets under $5 million. In the midrange are some fifty with assets of $50 million to $300 million. A few in the top range have assets up to a billion dollars.

The range of their performance is as wide as that of their assets. The great majority of family foundations simply distribute their few gifts to various local charities and churches that are of interest to the family members. Most have no full-time professional staff, although some of the larger and better-known family foundations are well staffed and carry on highly effective programs. Examples are the Mary Reynolds Babcock and the William Kenan in the Carolinas, the Nord and the Gund in Ohio, the Heinz in Pennsylvania, the Hall in Missouri, the Kempner in Texas, and the Dayton in Minnesota, all of which have been peaceful and productive, some over significant periods of time. At the other extreme there have been some miserably bad, even corrupt, family foundations. Among these are the Nemours Foundation of Alfred I. DuPont and the Moody in Texas, the all-time low. In between have been a great many whose programs have been useful enough but whose internal situation has gradually become one of stress and family conflict, particularly as control passes to the second and third generations.

The problems seem to be least severe in the great majority of smaller family foundations, that is, those with assets in the range of $1 million to $10 million, typically established by a donor who has been a successful doctor, lawyer, or corporation executive, or by the widow of such a person.

These facts about the sources of the modest wealth involved are important because of problems they do *not* create—namely, the divisive struggles that can attend the choosing of a successor to the donor in heading his or her substantial family company, or irresponsible behavior by children who have adopted the values and lifestyle of the spoiled and idle rich, or legal and personal struggles among the donor's descendants over control of a large body of foundation assets.

In fact, among smaller family foundations, a substantial subcategory in size, the donor generally is *not* torn by a retirement crisis, and the intention is generally to make modest grants to a familiar and often local list of the family's favorite charities. Family members participate in the infrequent and rather perfunctory board meetings to allocate the gifts largely out of a sense of duty. Quite often the family lawyer handles the administrative duties and keeps the records. Bank trust officers can also handle these duties, along with managing the investments.

As long as the donor is alive, in the typical case, things go smoothly enough, with much or little involvement of spouse and children, depending on his style. Once he has gone, his widow or the family lawyer may convene meetings and distribute the grants. But as the years pass, the children disperse to various new locations, their own families and activities preoccupy their attention, and the family foundation becomes a minor involvement if not a burden. The grandchildren tend to have even less interest. With the passage of years the donor will be a dim memory, and the foundation, if it still exists, will operate essentially out of a lawyer's or banker's file cabinet. There are many hundreds of such remnants around today.

A second important and more troubled subcategory of family foundations consists of those created by entrepreneurs who have made a considerable fortune by building a successful family firm— not a corner grocery or tailor shop, nor yet a large public corporation, but a profitable, substantial family enterprise. Such firms are an important element in the American economy, a major source of family wealth, and in philanthropic terms they are probably the source of most foundations in the $25 million to $100 million asset category.

Historically, the family firm and the family foundation were interlinked because of a huge loophole in the tax laws. Donors could give the ownership of their company to a foundation they created, take the full tax benefits, and name themselves and other family members as trustees. Then they could arrange that the foundation receive little, or even no, income from its company shareholdings—charity thus receiving little or no benefit.

A 1965 U.S. Treasury report found, after a study of some thirteen hundred of these foundations, that on average they reported less than half the rate of return on their concentrated holdings in the associated family company when compared to the returns reported by foundations with diversified holdings. And nearly half the foundations with concentrated shareholdings in the donor's company reported no income to the foundation whatever.

Quite apart from the losses to charity, such close linkages made these foundations a natural battleground for contests for control of the family business, which seriously damaged their effectiveness. These abuses were corrected by the Patman tax-reform legislation of 1969, and a major source of strife and damage to midsize family foundations was thereby eliminated.

Today the links between family firm and family foundation are much different but still extremely strong, primarily because the founder of the firm is most often also the founder of the foundation. A growing number of studies of family firms have revealed the enormous psychological and emotional problems such entrepreneurs face in deciding when and whether to retire from the firm and in choosing a successor. Indeed, conflicted feelings about letting go are so great that about three-quarters of family firms never do solve the succession problem and are either sold or liquidated after the founder's death or retirement. In the words of Massachusetts Institute of Technology professor Peter Senge, a well-known expert on these matters, "few corporations live even half as long as a person—most die before they reach the age of forty."

One element in this pattern of gridlock is that if the founder—most often a father—is to choose a successor, he must confront the painful fact of losing the base of his power, virtually of his identity. And if there is more than one child, and especially if there are two or more sons, the choice he makes can generate deep and enduring resentments. Not least, there is also his problem of deciding what to do with himself if he is no longer busy with the single greatest preoccupation and achievement of his life, namely the company he has built and led.

In any event, and whether or not he is able to solve the succession problem and save his company as an ongoing family enterprise, the dynastic-minded founder in a good many cases will establish a family-type foundation—perhaps as a part of his estate planning, perhaps as an alternative outlet for his energies, perhaps as a means of doing something for a favored cause. But all the old sentiments of blood and family, and all the hopes of remembrance and immortality will be present also, compounding the emotional complexity of his decisions.

If he does set up his family foundation while he is still alive and well, he will likely bring to it many of the same qualities—and faults—he displayed in the management of his company: close personal control of grant making and other decisions, a preponderant if not dominating presence at trustee meetings, and complicated relationships with the various other family members he has named to the board.

In the future, as women increasingly become entrepreneurs, senior corporate executives, and major investors, they may or may not display the same qualities and faults of the present generation of predominantly male donors.

The boards of family foundations tend to be weak and passive as long as the benefactor is alive. Once he or she is gone, if the spouse takes the chair, relative tranquillity may still prevail. But when the second generation finally takes over, disputes can surface, even erupt. Brothers and sisters, even in families with close ties, can still be extremely competitive with one another. In their role as members of the board of the family company, they may continue to compose or suppress their differences in order to minimize risks to the bottom line. But those same individuals, as trustees of the family foundation, rather frequently feel free to quarrel with one another vehemently—partly because grant-making issues seem to be more personal and value-laden, and partly perhaps because paralyzing family fights in the foundation arena give some emotional release without endangering the source of their wealth. As one despairing trustee of such a fractious foundation has said, "The trouble in a family like this is that everyone can afford his or her own lawyer and psychiatrist."

Considerable research has now been done on these behavior patterns. One of the leading centers of this work has been the Whitman Institute of San Francisco, which has compiled the following list of conflicts that can and commonly do arise, along with the underlying causes:

> power struggles between siblings, between generations, between branches of the family or between family factions; the refusal or reluctance of the older generation to hand over the reins to the next generation; long-standing hurts, grudges, and hostilities—spoken or unspoken—that result in lack of trust and respect; hidden agendas conceived to benefit a person, family branch or pet project; clashes of values, philosophy and politics in choosing projects to fund; different styles and ways of doing things; and male/female conflicts.

So widespread and consistent is the evidence of these problems that a number of initiatives in the foundation field have now been launched to try to alleviate them and attack the causes.

One approach is simply to increase communication among members of various family foundations to share experience and discuss remedies. The Council on Foundations, the mainline organization in the field, has now developed a rather extensive program of meetings among members of family foundations for this purpose. The Philanthropy Roundtable, a smaller organization with a conservative ideological tilt, carries on a similar effort for its supporters.

Another approach is semipsychiatric—to provide counseling to enable family members to get a better sense of their own motivations and conflicts and to understand the roots of the tensions. This has led to the production of a small but growing library of self-help books addressed to donors and to members of wealthy families. These texts offer counsel on how to head off problems and moderate the damaging consequences of conflicts.

A new small profession of specialized consultants and advisors to wealthy families with foundations has also now emerged to help them improve communication and collaboration with one another and to provide individual counseling. In addition, trust banks and investment firms have begun to offer special programs to attract families of wealth to place the endowments of their foundations with them for management. Gatherings of such family members are organized to discuss issues of common interest—ensuring trustee fidelity to the donor's intent, preparing third and fourth generations to be trustees—and hearing testimonials from members of well-functioning family foundations. Needless to say, the importance of sound handling of the assets of these foundations is not neglected in these discussions.

In the spirit of such occasions, the mood is emphatically upbeat. An example from the literature of one trust bank:

Family philanthropy becomes a legitimate and ennobling process, elevating the accident of kinship into the loftier realm of civic participation and responsibility. The often narrowing confines of individual giving open into the broadening vistas of social concern. . . . When a family investment in philanthropy is well executed, a family can achieve the cohesion that comes with a sense of higher purpose and cooperative effort. The educational experience of assessing public needs and evaluating grant proposals from the point of view of the public interest is an incomparable experience and one that can build strong bonds among family members.

Another example:

Family philanthropy offers an incomparable opportunity for individuals and families to do good by doing well. . . . Increased concentration of wealth in family foundations also helps shift the balance of philanthropic influence and responsibility away from government and gives individuals a chance to effect changes more directly and, perhaps, efficiently than would otherwise be possible.

To the extent that such uplifting assertions are taken seriously, they tend to obscure the very serious divisions and even disasters that now occur in many family foundations.

How successful or unsuccessful these various efforts are in alleviating some of the problems of family foundations—or possibly in creating unrealistic expectations on the part of families that create them—is not known. But a number of actual examples suggest that divisive tendencies within families may become more vivid and intense as the wealth involved is larger. The end result is that sizable family foundations, often after the sale or liquidation of the family company, become the primary arenas in which the competition or conflict among brothers and sisters and their spouses, and later among cousins and their spouses, takes place.

The Kirby, Cafritz, Scheuer, and Kerr foundations profiled in the next chapter are cases in point.

Chapter Twelve

—⸎—

The Acids
of Affluence

That family foundations often become cockpits of competition for control over family assets (and over the family company that generated those assets) provides one insight into the sociology of wealth in the United States. Furthermore, that they also rather frequently become theaters for deadly conflicts that have little to do with power and control of property, and much to do with emotions and personal hostilities, provides an additional insight into the psychopathology of inherited wealth in America.

Indeed it can be said that over the long term the greatest dangers to large family foundations derive from these acids of affluence. Their manifest effects on the successive generations of a wealthy founding family can include divorce, alcoholism, drugs, psychological problems, and personal irresponsibility engendered by inherited, unearned wealth.

The following four cases have in common substantial wealth, and the foundations all are into the second or third generation.

F. M. Kirby Foundation

The F. M. Kirby Foundation of New Jersey has assets of some $200 million. It was established by Fred Morgan Kirby, a cofounder of the F. W. Woolworth Company. He made his fortune from the success of that early five-and-dime chain-store operation. After his death his son, Allan Price Kirby, succeeded him as head of the foundation. Allan also later made his own mark in business by gaining control of a large railroad holding company, the Alleghany Corporation.

Allan was father of four children, two sons and two daughters. When he died in 1973, his only known letter on the subject of succession mentioned his hope that his descendants "down through the generations" would continue his work at the foundation. In somewhat cloudy circumstances his older son, Fred M. Kirby Jr., gained the controlling position over both the family foundation and the Alleghany Corporation, in which the family members had large shareholdings. Thereafter Alleghany prospered, eventually becoming a leading financial-services company under Fred Jr.'s clever management. Because its shares grew steadily in value, family discontent with his dominance tended to be allayed. But there was continuous tension on the board of the foundation, of which Fred Jr. was also chairman and on which his brother and two sisters also served. Animosity flared at times into active controversy over Fred's position.

In the spring of 1986 Fred informed the others by letter that he had, without their knowledge, installed his wife and children as "members" of the foundation who, by the two-tier arrangement set up in the charter, had the sole power to name trustees. When the others protested, he then removed his siblings as trustees, which produced a venomous family feud and years of litigation. Eventually the conflict spilled over onto the billion-dollar stage of the Alleghany Corporation as part of a struggle for its control.

The foundation became immobilized and the attorney general of New Jersey filed suit asking the courts to appoint a slate of independent trustees, partly on the grounds of alleged self-dealing and stock swapping between the foundation and Alleghany. Ultimately, the case reached the state supreme court, which ruled in 1990 that Fred's actions were in accordance with the foundation's charter. He is now in complete control.

The only consolation offered to the losers was this statement by the court: "In view of the blood ties between Fred and the Kirby plaintiffs, as well as the plaintiffs' years of service to the foundation, Fred's actions may well be viewed as exhibiting an unfortunate lack of tact and familial loyalty.... As long as his actions posed no threat to the Foundation, his status as member gave Fred the power to oust his siblings for any reason; or even for no reason at all."

Cafritz Foundation

The Cafritz Foundation of Washington, D. C., was established in 1962 by Morris Cafritz, an immigrant from Russia who became a wealthy real-estate developer in the nation's capital. In his forties he had married a nineteen-year-old Hungarian-American beauty, who became Washington's celebrity hostess in the 1940s and 1950s. In the words of a society columnist, "Where he was meat and potatoes, earnest frugality, and civic pride she was flashing dark beauty, mercurial moods and social ambition."

Cafritz set up the foundation to help various community organizations and the United Jewish Appeal. When he died shortly thereafter, his estate was the largest ever probated in the District of Columbia. He left half of it to the foundation and most of the rest to his wife, Gwendolyn.

As soon as she was in control of the foundation, its grants were increasingly focused on highbrow cultural causes—the Committee to Rescue Italian Opera, the Opera Society of Washington, the Corcoran Gallery, and the like.

Morris and Gwendolyn had three sons, all now wealthy businessmen. They all had difficult relationships with their mother. Unfortunately, after Morris' death Gwendolyn gradually sank more and more into alcoholism, and by the 1970s she had become a near-recluse. When she died in 1988, her last will left some $140 million to the foundation but nothing to her sons. She did stipulate, however, that one of them, Calvin, should serve on the foundation board.

Promptly, the other two sons sued to invalidate her will on grounds that she was mentally incompetent when she wrote it. Their motivation presumably was not money, of which both already had a great deal. One of them, it is believed, sought to take over control of the business empire his father founded, by gaining control of the foundation's large holdings of its shares.

The third son is married to a black woman, a local power in the arts and in liberal political causes. (Their daughter, Julia, has founded a rock group, called Pussy Galore, which has been described as "the gnarliest, most scuzzed-out molotov to hit the streets since the heady days of Teen Age Jesus and The Jerks." Most of the band's song titles are too profane for citation in mainstream reviews; one, a song that would surely have outraged the girl's grandfather, is titled, "You Look Like a Jew.")

One speculation is that the purpose of this third son is to use the

Cafritz endowment to give muscle to his wife's lifelong campaign to wrest the arts from the hands of Washington's white upper classes.

Relations within this family had been bad for a long time, since well before the litigation began. However the ongoing litigation eventually comes out, they are extremely unlikely to improve. But without doubt, the mother's act of discriminating against two of the children in her will detonated an explosion waiting to happen.

In this situation the foundation simply became an arena of controversy among the members of a shattered family, a casualty and not a potential vehicle of reconciliation.

S. H. and Helen R. Scheuer Family Foundation

The S. H. and Helen R. Scheuer Family Foundation of New York is among the two hundred largest in the country. For more than forty years it has had a commendable record of grant making, mainly to Jewish causes.

Simon Scheuer, the founder, was the descendant of German Jews who emigrated to the United States in the nineteenth century and became moderately wealthy. Si, as he was known, proved to be a canny investor, particularly in real estate. By the late 1940s he had amassed a large fortune, and the family foundation was created at that time.

Si and his wife, Helen, had five children, four sons and a daughter, who grew up in an environment of culture and great luxury. But the children also were taught that they had obligations to help the less fortunate. Their summers were usually spent working to improve the world—in the hills of Tennessee or in Mexico.

The children were very close. As a family friend said, "If you hung out with one, you hung out with all of them. They were very loving and supportive toward each other."

The mother was so absorbed with the children and family affairs that to her friends she often seemed to be out of touch with what was happening in the rest of the world. In later years her proudest possession was a charm bracelet inscribed with the initials and birth dates of her twenty-two grandchildren. Her own children all achieved distinguished careers—an award-winning film producer, a writer and TV personality, a psychotherapist, a member of Congress, and a very successful businessman. A clan, they have been almost a Jewish equivalent of the Kennedys or the Rockefellers.

But the fatal flaw in the unity of the dynasty was the character of their father. Si was a difficult man, short-tempered, tyrannical, and manipulative. One son said his father was "absurdly competitive with his male children." When one of them, James, made his first bid for a seat in Congress—with the endorsement of Eleanor Roosevelt and Averell Harriman, among others—his father publicly called him a "bum" and contributed to the campaign of his opponent.

Regarding the foundation, Si wrote that he thought its direction should be "entrusted to others than his immediate family, except for his wife." When he died, he created a field for strife and jealousy by settling far more money on his daughter than on his sons.

For some years after Si's death and as long as Helen was alive, the family still took vacations together, traveled abroad together, and celebrated the Jewish holidays together. But cracks in their solidarity were beginning to appear. Only the daughter and one of the brothers had been elected by the non-family members to the foundation board. So in 1980 the other siblings proposed that they all be made trustees. This suggestion was rejected. The daughter's husband was then elected to the board, which did nothing to ease resentments on the part of the excluded brothers. As tempers heated up, all the Scheuer siblings then did an extraordinary thing—they enrolled in a program for family counseling together. But in time that effort disintegrated.

In 1983 their mother died and their rivalries then exploded. Questions about the management of the foundation's assets by the non-family members were raised. Sharp differences over political and ideological questions developed between some of the non-family trustees and several of the non-trustee family members. In the words of one of them, "This isn't a fight about money, it is about how money is used."

Finally, in late 1989, all-out war was declared and a lawsuit was placed against the trustees by the excluded family members charging mismanagement and waste in the handling of the foundation's assets and conflicts of interest. Three of the trustees were also charged with criminal violations—coercion and bribery.

Steven, the son who is leading the attack, says, "This is an action both for and against my father. It's for him because he would be turning over in his grave if he could see the way his money's being wasted. And it's against him because the way he set up this foundation, he was trying to control things, to run people's lives the way he always did. I'm fighting a hand from the grave."

The Kerr Family Foundations

Robert S. Kerr, the son of a very poor tenant farmer in Oklahoma, was born at the end of the last century in a windowless log cabin. By his own talents and determination he became a lawyer and then a wealthy oilman and landowner. A huge man physically, and a witty and eloquent speaker, he turned to politics, winning the governorship of his home state and then a seat in the U.S. Senate in 1948. He soon became one of the Senate's most-powerful members. His influence was especially great on agriculture and minerals policies, flood control, Social Security, tax policy, and ultimately the space program.

In 1952 Kerr made a run for the Democratic presidential nomination, but he could not overcome his image as a provincial, special-interests politician, and his effort failed. Thereafter he devoted himself to Oklahoma rather than national concerns, and to his business affairs. He died suddenly and prematurely in early 1963, without having prepared a plan for the disposition of his large fortune.

Within the year, his widow, Grayce B. Kerr, created the Kerr Foundation with the advice of a long-time family friend and business associate, James Webb, a prominent Washington figure who had headed the National Aeronautics and Space Agency during the Kennedy administration. Initially endowed with some $14 million, the foundation focused on the problems of Oklahoma, especially the needs of farm and ranch families. It sponsored special agricultural demonstration programs and somewhat later created an economic studies program to assist in the planning of the state's future social and economic development.

In form it was a family foundation, and the mother, the four Kerr children, and their spouses were named as "life trustees." At Webb's urging, it was envisaged that the foundation would eventually become a "public" institution with non-family trustees in the majority. Several non-family "term trustees" were added, all of them individuals of high standing. Thus the foundation was thoughtfully constructed and was directed to broad and important purposes consistent with the donor's intentions. Nonetheless, it all unraveled within twenty years.

The usual suspects—too much money, sibling rivalry, gradually diverging interests, divorces and remarriages, and the strong tendency of wealth to induce addictions, behavioral aberrations, and irresponsibility—before long produced their destructive effects. The children had been both babied and bullied in growing up. The senator, a dominating personality, was all-controlling in the family's affairs until he died—"even to designating which seats they had to sit in during airplane trips," as one close friend has said. The children were not expected to pursue serious careers on their own, and none did, not even by taking positions in the family company. Among the grandchildren few have ever finished college or taken gainful employment.

Divorces were also epidemic, and in some way they triggered the breakdown of the foundation as it was originally envisaged. The second son, Breene Kerr, served as chair of the board for the first fourteen years, and he managed to maintain an adequate degree of family collaboration. Then he left the chairmanship for a period. In his absence large changes were made toward converting the foundation into the kind of public institution James Webb had long advocated, including the naming of a non-family chairman and the appointment of a new president, who promptly introduced significant program changes.

Breene Kerr then resumed active status on the board, having been through a divorce and remarriage. At that point there were three new spouses among Senator Kerr's children, all of whom wanted to become trustees. By this time discontent was evident among some family members over the rate at which family influence was being diluted. As a reflection of this concern, the three new spouses were elected to the board, effectively reversing the foundation's evolution toward public status.

Over the next three years, between 1982 and 1985, the Kerr Foundation continued to function as a single entity, but with increasing strains and frictions within the family. Gradually the trustees realized that their interests had become more and more diverse and in some cases were no longer centered on Oklahoma. Ultimately the board came to the conclusion that they no longer could nor wanted to function as a family unit.

As a result, with the help of family attorneys, they reached an agreement to divide the foundation into four equal parts. In early 1986, after gaining Internal Revenue Service approval, four new entities came into existence. The Kerr Center for Sustainable Agriculture, headed by Kay Kerr Adair, carries on some of the agricultural and environmental projects that Senator Kerr began. The Kerr Foundation, Inc., the Robert S. and Grayce B. Kerr Foundation, and the Grayce B. Kerr Fund, Inc., are each headed by one of the senator's three sons. All work in somewhat similar fields of education, cultural activities, and human services. These independent grant-making foundations have separate offices and staffs, and they have no overlapping trustees. The clearest result of this restructuring has been an end to the family's philanthropic struggles. The four foundations are now operating without serious internal tensions, and it appears that once released from the pressures of "forced cooperation" within a single family entity, relationships among the family members have improved to the point that several cases of cooperative grant making have happened between their separate foundations.

However, resolution of the foundation's tensions has not resolved the deeper personal problems of some members of the family. The new challenge, in the words of one observer, is "to teach the younger Kerrs how to be responsible foundation members when they are still struggling with responsibility in real life."

The Kerr foundations are an instructive example of a surgical solution to family philanthropic problems that have gone beyond the reach of communication and compromise. Compared to the previous situation of turmoil and deadlock, the solution reached represents a definite gain in terms of the public interest and probably family relationships as well.

A time may come in any family foundation, when factions have formed, that the members should recognize that it is better to go their separate ways than to go on quarreling endlessly. To remind himself of this, Curtis Meadows Jr., the highly respected head of the Meadows Foundation in Dallas, Texas, never forgets the Biblical story of Abram and Lot in Genesis 13:

> Now Abram was very rich in cattle, in silver, and in gold.... And Lot, who went with Abram, also had flocks and herds and tents, so that the land could not support both of them dwelling together, and there was strife between the herdsmen of Abram's cattle and the herdsmen of Lot's cattle.... Then Abram said to Lot, "Let there be no strife between you and me ... for we are kinsmen.... Is not the whole land before you? Separate yourself from me. If you take the left hand, then I will go to the right, or if you take the right hand, I will go to the left." ... So Lot chose for himself all the Jordan valley, and Lot journeyed east; thus they separated from each other. Abram dwelt in the land of Canaan, while Lot dwelt among the cities of the valley.

Meadows also keeps on his desk a quotation from a less-eminent source, Ross Perot: "Every good and excellent thing stands moment by moment on the razor's edge of danger and must be fought for."

For a good many American family foundations, the wisdom of both the Bible and Perot are worth remembering. It is also worth remembering that there are a few family foundations that for a considerable period of time—that is, two or three generations—have remained peaceful and productive. One of these is the Mary Reynolds Babcock Foundation of North Carolina, founded in

1953. Its history and the methods by which it has operated are instructive and give encouragement that some of the hazards that imperil family foundations may be manageable.

Mary Reynolds Babcock Foundation

Mary Reynolds Babcock was one of the daughters of R. J. Reynolds, one of the earliest and greatest of the tobacco kings. He and his wife were themselves charitable individuals, and they left an enduring charitable tradition. All in all the several branches of the family have now created some eleven foundations that have distributed more than $500 million to date in gifts and grants in the Carolinas and other southeastern states.

At her death Mary Reynolds Babcock set up the foundation that bears her name. In the trust indenture she stated its sweeping objective: "To improve the human condition the world over," and she left wide latitude for the judgment and discretion of the trustees in carrying out that mandate. They subsequently decided to focus the foundation's work in the southeastern United States and on the problems of education and the arts.

The board was to be made up of both family and non-family members, and the practice was established early and followed consistently of appointing outstanding individuals with experience in philanthropy to the non-family seats. One of these trustees, the late Paul Ylvisaker, well known in foundation work, considered this practice to be very important. In his view, the presence of "non-family members at the family dinner table improves everyone's behavior."

One of the original and most active trustees was the donor's daughter, Katy Mountcastle. Under her, several beneficial principles in the operation of the foundation were firmly established:

First, projects that were to be funded were to be decided by the board as a whole. Individual projects and pet family projects were to be kept to a minimum.

Second, the board was to participate fully in deciding on the projects funded. Trustees were to make site visits and report their observations and judgments back to the entire board as a basis for its final decision. The practice of making grant decisions by the board as a whole produced, in effect, a level and neutral playing field in which non-family and family members felt equal responsibility and influence.

Third, a policy was followed of appointing a strong executive director for the foundation from outside the family. This further reinforced the principle of collaborative, independent judgment in grant making.

There was also an external factor that probably influenced the foundation beneficially. When the Reynolds Tobacco Company had grown from a family firm into a large publicly held corporation, the appointment of non-family leadership in its ranks happened early on. The effect of this as far as the foundation was concerned was to eliminate one of the common sources of friction and division on a family board, namely competition among members for control of the associated family firm.

These are among the identifiable elements that have enabled the Mary Reynolds Babcock Foundation to build a singularly good record and reputation over the past forty years, but two intangible factors may also have been operative.

First, the donor came from a family with long experience in and dedication to philanthropy. From the start the policies introduced by her into in the foundation's operation were not those of an amateur or dilettante.

A second and even less tangible element that may have contributed to the foundation's continuity and effectiveness is what could be called the "philanthropic ethos" of the Carolinas, as exemplified by the Dukes, the Kenans, and other notable donors of the region. On the whole these benefactors seem to have avoided the worst tendencies of some foundation builders in other regions— Texas, California, and parts of the Midwest, for example.

This is purely suppositional of course, but so many mysterious factors (including sheer chance) seem to play a role in the fate and performance of some foundations that something like regional ethos, despite its intangibility, should not necessarily be dismissed out of hand.

A final note: Paul Ylvisaker, who played a long and significant part in the good performance of this foundation (and many others), nonetheless remained of the opinion that some 50 percent of family foundations will probably run into serious problems within a generation or two and that these problems increase dramatically after the third generation. Shortly before his death he predicted that virtually every family-type foundation in the United States will have broken up or faced disastrous difficulties before it is a century old. This rather directly leads to the subject of community foundations and their potentialities.

Chapter Thirteen

—⚜—

Community Foundations

A Great Invention

The very broad impulse of wealthy Americans to establish a family foundation is an understandable and admirable reflection of a national philanthropic spirit. Some 75 percent of all American foundations are of this type. Yet it is a serious national problem that so many such foundations are torn apart by family tensions or fall into decay from neglect within two or three generations.

Counseling, mediation, and the subdivision of these fragile creations may provide a partial solution to these problems. Another measure widely resorted to, when disputes and differences have become irreconcilable, is simply to transfer the remaining assets of the foundation in the form of one or more capital gifts to operating nonprofits such as a university or hospital, then to shut the foundation down. But an alternative to the traditional family foundation that is increasingly turned to is the transfer of the assets to what is known as a "community foundation." In fact, this has now become a major national movement in philanthropy, one with vast positive potential.

In the saga of American philanthropy there have been several great and unexpected breakthroughs and cleansings—from the invention of the large, professionalized grant-making foundation in the early twentieth century to the Patman reforms of 1969. But among these one of the most valuable inventions relating to family foundations has been the community foundation, created in the early years of the twentieth century.

Its inventor, Frederick Goff, was a prominent lawyer and civic leader in Cleveland, Ohio. Concerned about the stagnant assets in private charitable trusts, Goff sought a legal means of breaking the grip of "the dead hand" over such trusts that had lost their usefulness with the passage of time. Illustrative of these was Ben Franklin's early nineteenth-century fund established to help worthy apprentices; by the end of that century apprentices had largely disappeared from the American economy, making the trust superfluous. Yet by the usual legal procedures, it was long and laborious to modify original trusts, no matter how irrelevant they had become.

Goff was obsessed with the thought that tens of millions of dollars of social capital were being left to molder because of the "dead hand rule," known in legal doctrine as the *cy pres doctrine*. Seeking a solution that would make those funds available for useful purposes, he discussed the problem with almost every banker, lawyer, public official, and business person he met in cities across the country.

The formula he finally devised was as simple as it was sensible. A new type of foundation directed by a partnership between trustee banks and a responsible group of citizen leaders would be formed. It would provide unified management for a number of charitable trusts. When leaving their endowments to the foundation, donors would agree that their charitable directives would be honored so long as they were not obsolete or harmful and that their objectives could be altered by the foundation's directors as changing circumstances might require, without resort to the courts.

In sum, Goff conceived a new kind of foundation headed by a board of eminent local citizens authorized to receive such endowments, to update the purposes of the trusts, and when necessary to direct their grants to new and more relevant purposes. The investment of the transferred funds would be administered by one or a group of leading local banks. The power to make grants from the income received would be in the hands of a distribution committee made up of prominent local citizens appointed by leading local figures such as a state or federal judge, a university president, or a head of the local medical association. An annual public report of grants and an annual audit were other important elements of the plan.

Having invented the concept of the community foundation, Goff built a working model in Cleveland. Launched in 1914, it got off to a promising start. Then, indefatigably, Goff took his "Cleveland Plan" around the country to get it adopted. During 1915 alone, a year after the founding of the Cleveland Community Foundation, eight new community foundations came into existence.

The community foundation idea spread gradually to other cities and held particular attraction for new smaller and midsize donors. It offered them the benefit and inducement of the services of an eminent board, competent professional staff, and trustworthy handling of the endowment. Very important, the original purposes could readily be updated from time to time as changed circumstances required.

The idea caught on, and today there are about 350 community foundations. They exist in every part of the country, and their assets total some $9 billion dollars, derived from eighteen thousand individual and family gifts. Indeed, the spread of the idea has gone beyond anything Goff could have hoped for, and the functions that community foundations now serve go far beyond the removal of the "dead hand control" over stagnant private trusts—which was Goff's original concern.

The forces powering this extraordinary growth in community foundations are only gradually coming to be understood. One is the simple convenience in the formation of a family philanthropy. All the legal, organizational, and financial arrangements necessary to set up a new independent foundation are simplified. In an attractive form of one-stop shopping, one buys into an existing, ongoing institution, and at the same time one receives all the tax benefits given to an ordinary charitable contribution.

A second factor is the solidity and security of the institution to which the funds are being committed: the high standing of the members of the board, the typically good grant-making record and reputation of the local community foundation over time, and assurance that the local foundation is part of a strong and respected national movement. All of those factors are powerfully attractive to family members seeking a respected and reliable institution in which to place their philanthropic funds.

A third element that is reassuring in the community foundation movement is the involvement of the leading local banks in the handling of the foundation's investments. This adds to the feeling that the institution is honorable, reliable, competent, durable—all psychologically important in any family's decision to transfer ultimate and permanent control over a portion of their wealth.

A fourth factor is the competence of the local foundation's staff and its reputation in the community. Unlike the great national foundations, whose activities are only vaguely familiar to a widely dispersed public, community foundations are continuously under the gaze of an attentive local public—a very important feedback process and disciplinary influence.

The evolution over time of several donor options—permanent and nonpermanent funds, "field of interest" funds, and "donor advised funds"—have all been responsive to the interests of various donors and have increased the attractiveness of the community foundation in the decisions of a growing number of grantor families.

There are still other powerful but intangible attractions of Goff's idea to potential donors. Creating a named family fund in a community foundation has now achieved the dignity and status of a recognized memorial. Because the foundation is community-based, the idea draws on a powerful motivating psychological factor, namely the strong identification and affection of a family for its own locality, its roots.

The basic trade-off is that donors have to give up ultimate ownership and control of the funds they commit to the community foundation, and for some this is a deterrent. On the other hand, because of the genius of Goff's original concept, the donor to a community foundation is buying into the priceless and very reassuring values of institutional reputation, professional competence and responsibility, and institutional durability.

Over time, Goff's original plan has been refined and additional advantages and inducements have been developed. Funds can now be given for designated purposes and can carry the donor's or the donor family's name, thus accommodating name-recognition or memorial interests. More recently, "donor advised funds" make it possible for donors or their family to play an advisory role in the distribution of grants from the funds they have provided. Thus families have a satisfying degree of participation in the grant-making process.

The community foundation concept does not meet all the needs of every donor family, but it meets most of the needs and concerns of a great many, the evidence for which is the continuing vigorous growth of the movement.

Because of the success of community foundations, a few derivatives have now been developed, most of them also growing quite vigorously. These include similar collective philanthropic initiatives centering on a specific ethnic or religious group. The United Jewish Appeal–Federation of Jewish Philanthropies, for example, has developed major initiatives of this kind.

Similarly, there is now a vigorous spread of new women's foundations, and also a growing number focusing on a particular problem or cause—the environment, the problems of children, or the reform of education. All of these offer the same essential advantages to the donor: full tax benefits, simplicity and convenience, and the opportunity to buy into an experienced nonprofit organization carrying on a program focused on a problem or issue of special interest to the donor.

The traditional family foundation, with all its possible problems and inconveniences is still, statistically, the preferred philanthropic vehicle for the majority of wealthy American families. But the community foundation, with its variations and derivatives, is now a proven and increasingly favored vehicle for such donors. Among its broad social benefits is that it has opened the door to vastly increased participation in the national philanthropic tradition for a huge segment of the American population that embraces 20 to 25 percent of the population just below the richest 5 percent. This important contribution to the democratization of American philanthropy fills the space between the millions of ordinary givers to charity, on the one hand, and independent foundation founders on the other.

But do community foundations also provide a solution to or an escape from the accumulating tensions and eventual self-destructiveness of so many family-type foundations in the long run? This is a more complex and difficult question because it relates to that vast and mysterious realm of the psychological and emotional factors involved in the processes of wealth holding, transference, and inheritance—and the impact of unearned wealth on human and family behavior.

Somehow when the members of a family are in direct and total control of a family-type foundation, passions are often aroused, factions develop, old wounds in relationships are reopened, and the foundation becomes an arena not of healing collaboration but of bitter, even deadly, conflict. On the other hand, donor-advised funds administered by community foundations typically do not.

Why then is the relinquishment of ultimate control over inherited wealth to a community foundation such a trauma for some family members? And once the commitment of such wealth to a community foundation is made, why does the interposition of a professional staff and a larger structure of control over the transferred wealth so often defuse those family tensions? Does the very presence of neutral, competent, nonthreatening individuals inhibit the family maneuvering and outbreaks? Is there indeed a kind of inhibitory embarrassment about fighting in the presence of strangers? Or does the transfer of ultimate ownership and control of the funds from family hands to the community foundation somehow make power plays and the drive of family factions for dominance irrelevant?

Whatever the operative forces may be, the evidence is compelling that family participation in the procedures of community-foundation grant making typically produces a more collaborative pattern of family behavior. Given the huge number of family foundations and their many problems, the growing number and the variety of community and affinity-group foundations have to be regarded as a major, heartening development.

Part Six

—ᏋᏋᏋ—

*Entrepreneurial
Philanthropy*

Chapter Fourteen

—⚜—

Mission-Driven, High-Impact Foundations

In the saga of American philanthropy there have been wise, purposeful, and highly successful donors of various kinds, both men and women; there have been failures and near failures; and there have been the many family foundations, untroubled and troubled. But there has also been a special group of entrepreneurial donors—individuals who brought to their philanthropy not only their wealth but also their creative business skills, their negotiating talents, and their zeal and energy. As a result, they have been able to multiply the impact of their gifts manyfold. They are surprisingly few, given the large American entrepreneurial class. Nevertheless they represent a special kind of achievement in philanthropy to which many other donors, even those of modest wealth, might aspire.

The Rouses and the Enterprise Foundation

In his business career James Rouse was extraordinarily successful in commercial real estate. The Rouse Company is a nationally known developer of shopping malls, festival markets such as South Street Seaport in New York, and new planned communities such as Columbia, Maryland, which continues to be Rouse's base of operations.

James Rouse and his wife, Patty, had long been active in charitable and religious work, and in the 1970s they became involved in a program sponsored by the Church of the Savior in Washington, D.C., to rehabilitate deteriorated apartment buildings in a run-down section of the city. The residents would then be assisted in managing the buildings, learning new skills, and finding employment.

The success of that project caused the Rouses to believe that what had been accomplished in Washington could be replicated elsewhere. So in 1982 they founded the Enterprise Foundation with the visionary national objective of "giving all low income people the opportunity to have fit and affordable housing and to get out of poverty into the mainstream of American life."

A few years later Jim retired from his company to devote himself full-time to the foundation's agenda. He brought to that new mission the fruits of his years of successful experience as a major builder—his familiarity with the financial, managerial, and legal aspects of community development; his vast network of friends in business, government and banking; and his great entrepreneurial talents. He has applied these intangible assets energetically, together with a significant portion of his family's wealth, to the new Rouse crusade.

A first step was to build a board of some of the most eminent, experienced, and influential Americans from government, banking, philanthropy, and the field of low-income housing. Members included Robert McNamara, former U. S. secretary of defense; James A. Johnson, head of Fannie Mae; John Gardner, founder of Independent Sector; Ronald Grzynski, head of Shorebank Corporation in Chicago; and Cushing Dolbeare, president of the National Low Income Housing Coalition—plus several former congressmen and senators who had played key roles in the formulation of national housing policies over the years.

With the help and guidance of that powerful group, plus Rouse's driving energy, Enterprise Foundation became a national force within a decade. It has not yet reached its ambitious national objective, but it has made a considerable beginning.

Now working with more than five hundred neighborhood groups and partnerships in 153 locations across the country, Enterprise has helped to produce more than 36,300 homes since 1981. These groups are provided with loans and grants to get their projects started, and they are given help in learning how to rehabilitate and construct housing at the lowest cost, how to finance and manage low-income housing projects, how to carry on their own fund-raising, and how to address problems of education, health care, and employment and training that are central to the lives of low-income citizens.

Thus far, Enterprise has raised over $32 million to support its program. To help local groups in funding their projects, it has developed a number of innovative ideas including the recruitment of thousands of "benevolent lenders"—that is, well-to-do suburban church members willing to help finance inner-city housing projects with loans below market rates, often as low as 2 percent. It has also initiated the syndication of low-income housing mortgages in order to tap the resources of the financial markets, and it has helped local groups raise about $300 million in loans from some seventy major corporations.

To carry out special tasks, Enterprise has spawned various new subsidiaries. One of these is the National Center for Lead-Safe Housing to develop strategies for sharply reducing childhood lead poisoning. At the same time the center helps preserve the nation's stock of affordable housing, since one of the major reasons private landlords are abandoning low-income properties is the prohibitive cost of lead-paint abatement. Another Enterprise subsidiary is the Enterprise Social Investment Corporation, established to help non-profit organizations raise equity capital for housing projects. Yet another is the Housing Outreach Fund, a partnership with Fannie Mae specifically to provide equity to smaller housing developments, which often have the greatest difficulty attracting capital.

An eloquent speaker and advocate, Rouse has indefatigably toured the nation's city halls, city councils, state legislatures, foundations, and corporate board rooms to give visibility to the issues of housing the nation's poor. As co-chair of the National Housing Task Force, he has also played an influential role in persuading Congress to introduce various needed changes in low-income housing legislation.

Thinking further into the future, Rouse has now also created the Enterprise Development Company as a potentially profit-making arm of the foundation. When the Development Company begins to turn a profit, the funds will flow into the Enterprise Foundation. In effect, it will then become a money machine for the enduring support of the foundation's efforts.

Jim and Patty, full partners in all these undertakings, made some stumbles at the start while they learned about the special needs and complications of low-income neighborhoods. But they learned quickly, and their Enterprise Foundation has now become an important source of financial and technical assistance to such distressed areas nationwide. For both of them, their crusade to improve the conditions of the poor has been a dramatically new and invigorating career.

Fred Braun and Prison Labor

Fred P. Braun of Kansas is a Harvard Business School graduate who made himself a millionaire by the time he was forty, sold his metal-products company, and then began to look for some kind of public service he could devote himself to. First he ran for public office in his home state and lost twice. Then in the early 1970s the governor named him to a task force to improve the management of state agencies and he was assigned to review the operations of the penal system. From that experience he found his mission—namely, to apply his business skills to helping solve a major social problem—and he has dedicated his time and energy to prison reform ever since.

In the course of his first visits to the prisons Braun was shocked to discover that the great majority of inmates were idle most of the time. They did not make license plates, or work on the prison farm, or learn any skills in training programs. The few hours they were "busy" were spent picking up paper or cleaning the kitchen. The rest of the time they spent lying on their backs watching television.

"I began to see why these guys are worse off when they get out than when they went in," said Braun, "intellectually, emotionally and physically."

So he decided that what was needed was a new kind of company located near a prison, where inmates could get on a bus, go to a real job, work a full day side by side with non-inmates, make some money, develop some pride, and be in a position, when they had served their time, to function in normal society.

He also decided that all the disciplines of a profit-making company had to operate. It would not be good enough to build such a company as a new kind of social welfare agency. It had to be a realistic work experience that would prepare the inmate for the real world.

In his zeal—and his innocence—Braun had no idea at the start that by his radical and visionary concept he was bucking history, laws, public prejudices, governmental bureaucracy, and the vested interests of both business and labor. Inmate labor in the United States has long been regarded as "a species of slavery, degrading to the criminal, demoralizing to the honest manufacturers, and causing paupers of free labor," as the AFL declared at its founding in 1881. One hundred years later such attitudes were still common and had been embodied in laws in more than thirty states restricting the hiring of prisoners and the sale of prison-made goods.

Braun was also initially ignorant of the fact that because of these multiple problems and risks, not a single one of this nation's forty thousand foundations, many of which claim they are innovative and risk-taking, had ever tackled the task of prisoner job training and ultimate civilian employability in a practical way. Before the inherently difficult task of launching a new business and making it viable could even be addressed, the legal and bureaucratic problems, the obstacles of public attitudes and resistance, and the opposition of various vested interests all had to be dealt with.

Therefore Braun began by talking privately with influential individuals throughout Kansas, most of whom were initially skeptical if not actually opposed to his idea. He then talked with state po-

litical leaders and corrections officials and got some encouragement. He was also encouraged by the passage by Congress of an act
in 1979 permitting private companies to hire inmates under certain
strict conditions and permitting the sale of inmate-made goods in
interstate commerce.

He then traveled the state of Kansas explaining the potential advantages of his idea in terms of reducing the heavy costs of the
penal system, gaining tax revenues, and advancing prison reform.
Little by little he won support from both business and community
leaders. He also talked to inmates and prison guards and aroused
their interest in his idea. He discussed it with various nonprofit and
public service groups and got their blessing. Only the trade union
leaders remained negative after the first year of these preparatory
consultations.

Next Braun formed a private, profit-oriented company, Creative
Enterprises, Inc. Its advisory committee included a Kansas state
senator, the director of the Kansas Correctional Institution for
Women, a cofounder of the Black Awareness Program at the state
penitentiary, members of the media, University of Kansas faculty,
union representatives, and others.

At this point, after two years of dogged effort, Braun and his co-
directors could finally confront a series of basic business decisions:
What type of business should be started or purchased? Where
could it be located? What legal problems had to be overcome to
permit paid employment for prisoners working for a private company? How could the rules of the associated prison be modified to
meet the work schedule and other needs of the company? What
community opposition might there be to the idea of transporting
convicted felons daily to work outside prison walls, and how could
it be dealt with?

Ultimately Braun decided to purchase a troubled sheet-metal factory located in an adjacent state, partly because he had successful business experience in that field and partly because bringing in an out-of-state company lessened the concern of union leaders that it would displace local workers. It would be located in Leavenworth, Kansas, a town that was already the location of state, federal, and military prisons and was receptive to the new project. The plant would have a work force that was half inmate and half civilian. This added some complications but was considered to be important in creating a realistic work environment. The inmates would work regular hours, would be transported to and from the prison daily by bus, and would be accompanied by a prison guard. They would be paid prevailing wages, from which up to 80 percent could be deducted for taxes, room and board at the prison, family support, and victims' compensation. The remainder they could save or spend. The plant would have an open-door policy so community, labor, business, media, and others could visit and reassure themselves that there were no violations of commitments.

Braun had to provide or guarantee a large part of the financing for the venture, and he ultimately had to take over direct management. During the following years a long succession of new problems had to be overcome—developing a marketable line of products, maintaining high-quality controls, and fitting together the two basically different sets of rules of a prison and a manufacturing company. But these were all dealt with, and the enterprise survived.

Over its first decade the original venture, called Zephyr Products Co., made a profit in some years, incurred losses in another, and overall had a small net gain. It employed more than two hundred inmates, who earned total wages of $1,650,000 and repaid more than 40 percent of their wages "to society." Most of the remainder of their earnings went into personal savings. Each employee was paid the federal minimum wage of $3.80 per hour plus a performance bonus. They were also full participants in the Employee Stock Ownership Plan.

Based on the lessons learned from the first venture, a second company, Heatron, Inc., was started in 1985, also in Leavenworth. It manufactures electrical heating elements. In its first five years Heatron employed about one hundred inmates, who collectively earned $700,000 in wages. Forty-three percent of their earnings were "returned" in the form of taxes and other repayments. Like Zephyr Products, the Heatron initiative has not requested nor received any governmental funds or subsidies.

A milestone was reached in March 1991 when a symbolic check for $1 million was presented to the taxpayers of Kansas, representing the savings to them as a result of the Braun projects.

Creative Enterprises has maintained contact with all previous inmate-employees and traced their employment records. "We believe our recidivism rate is about 50 percent of the normal rate," Braun reports. "When they get out, they have jobs, confidence, money and contacts—which is a good way to stay out." The inmates confirm Braun's favorable judgment. One said, for example, "This has been a chance to replace empty days and to prepare ourselves to return to society. I don't want to mess up this program for everybody else who's worked so hard to make it go."

Most recently, after his years of experience with Zephyr and Heatron, and once they became modestly profitable, Braun decided to sell these enterprises to new owners who would continue their operation. This he did in order to turn his attention to multiplying the program by encouraging and financing other owners to create new Zephyrs and Heatrons. As his vehicle he recently created the Workman Foundation, aiming to support some fifty new companies with investments of $200,000 each that would provide as many as 4,500 full-time jobs for inmates. A new garment-sewing plant employing inmates has already been funded in Utah, and Braun has bought a bankrupt snowplow plant in Iowa, which he plans to move to Leavenworth. More projects are under study.

The path Braun is breaking is still steep and rough, but he says that as long as he can just break even, he will continue his efforts because of the personal satisfaction they bring. This has been his main reward for his labors. In his words: "When I talk to my Harvard Business School classmates, they joke about these companies and want to know how I could be dumb enough to lose all that money. But then they say, 'Fred, you had the courage to break away. We wish we could do that. But we're caught up in the rat race of making more and more and more money.'

"It's nice to hear that from your peers," Braun concludes. "That's gratification."

More recently this once-lonesome advocate for what at first was regarded as a hopeless cause, finally got some public recognition as well. He received the "1993 Socially Responsible Entrepreneur of the Year Award" from an assemblage of Kansas City's most prominent business leaders.

The John M. Olin Foundation

Among these mission-driven foundations the Olin Foundation has pursued the most ambitious and intangible quest of all, namely, to change the prevailing political climate in the United States from one which the donor viewed as dangerously infected with ideas of socialism to one with a commitment to "freedom of enterprise."

Other wealthy Americans have tried through their philanthropy to protect and build support for the American enterprise system, most of them with little success, but generally their efforts were amateurish and episodic, often mere expressions of personal resentments or simply ballyhoo for business that persuaded no one.

For example, Alfred P. Sloan, the great builder of General Motors, after being stung by an attack of the Roosevelt administration for tax evasion, set up his foundation to "battle American economic illiteracy." But what was produced was mainly a series of propaganda pamphlets and films based largely on the writings of Robert Welch, founder of the John Birch Society, that appealed almost exclusively to the far right. After a brief and embarrassing interval, the effort was abandoned.

In the early 1960s the Lilly family of Indiana, angered by Senator Estes Kefauver's investigations of the pharmaceutical industry, became involved briefly (through their foundation) with a campaign to promote "better understanding of the anticommunist free enterprise limited government concept." But this led to entanglements with the Christian Anti-Communist Crusade and the John Birch Society, and the effort was soon allowed to expire.

H. L. Hunt, the Texas oil billionaire, was vehemently for free enterprise and against Communism and socialism. But his donations were mainly in the form of free airplane travel for Senator Joseph McCarthy and for the publication and dissemination of the views of racists and other scurrilous extremists.

Over the past thirty years that kind of crude and mindless propaganda has been displaced by a sustained and sophisticated assault by a group of foundations on the pretensions and premises of American liberalism, including its economic, political, and cultural aspects. This has played a significant part in bringing about a marked shift in the intellectual and political climate of the United

States. In that transformation, the John M. Olin Foundation has taken a key role.

John Olin, the founder, was a man of many talents and interests. He was born into an old and well-established family that owned a profitable company manufacturing gunpowder and ammunition. He was trained as a chemist and over time won some twenty patents for his discoveries in the improvement of explosives and ammunition. After his father's death he became head of the family business and developed it into the vast Olin Industries Corporation, a producer of industrial chemicals, aluminum, arms and ammunition, timber, paper, and other products.

Among his various nonprofit affiliations, Olin was an active conservationist and also served as a trustee of Cornell and of Johns Hopkins University during the student upheavals of the 1960s. He was in his sixties when he found the great cause to which he was to devote the last phase of his life, namely, "seeing free enterprise reestablished in this country." In his view, business and the public "had to be awakened to the creeping stranglehold that socialism has gained here since World War II." He energetically devoted his efforts to that objective during the last quarter-century of his long life, and through his foundation he gave the cause a large portion of his wealth.

Olin's timing in launching his crusade was just right. To understand why that was so, it is useful to look at the political climate in Europe after the end of World War II and at the career of an American named Irving Kristol. At that time the influence of Communist organizations and socialist ideology was very great, even dominant on the Continent; and it was in Europe that the major intellectual counteraction, or counterattack, began. One important element in that nascent movement was a CIA-funded organization, the Congress for Cultural Freedom, which provided a gathering point for many of the most distinguished non-Communist European intellectuals. The Congress also subsidized a group of new and influential intellectual journals in non-Communist countries.

One of these journals, *Encounter,* was published in Britain and was edited by the English poet Stephen Spender and Irving Kristol. The latter was a former Trotskyite, educated at City College in New York, who had been involved from his school days in intense political and ideological debate. A brilliant writer and speaker, Kristol also had a genius for forming strong networks of like-minded intellectuals. Through *Encounter* and its contributors and subscribers, a fierce intellectual battle with Communism and socialism was joined. Within a few years, by the sheer brilliance and quality of their attacks, the journal's rather small group of contributors gained great influence, which quickly spread from purely academic and intellectual circles to the media, labor and business organizations, and also to the sphere of politics.

Their efforts also began to have resonance in intellectual circles in the United States so that by the end of the 1950s Kristol had decided to leave England and continue his campaign at home, bringing with him his firm conviction that the major and deep shifts in politics and the political atmosphere begin in the debates of small circles of dedicated and articulate intellectuals.

Even before his return, events were happening that would offer opportunities for Kristol's initiative. The old brand of American anti-Communism, in the wake of the ugly McCarthy excesses, had largely lost its public standing. But the writings of such writers as Alexander Solzhenitsyn and Theodore Draper were exposing the horrors of the Soviet system. William Buckley was publishing his new *National Review*, the Baroodys (father and son) were transforming the American Enterprise Institute into a vigorous and sophisticated public-policy center in Washington, and a few foundations like the Smith-Richardson and the Sarah Scaife were funding some of the new conservative voices.

Still Kristol's return made an important difference. He found financial backing to establish a new journal, *The Public Interest*, which quickly gained influence as he gathered about him an array of remarkable writers and intellectuals. Indeed he found himself, somewhat to his surprise, the acknowledged godfather of the surging new political movement called Neoconservatism, which in time helped shape to a significant degree the policies of three administrations, those of Presidents Nixon, Reagan, and Bush.

During the 1960s, as the Neoconservative movement began to form, the Olin Foundation under the donor's personal direction, joined its ranks. Gradually the foundation increased its initially modest grants to the cause, and by the mid-1970s it was distributing $1 million a year in a pattern that reflected a keen awareness of the more important conservative scholars and writers who were then emerging. The grant list was selective and of high-quality, although it did not yet seem to be based on a carefully planned strategy.

By 1980 the grants of the foundation had tripled, and a young protégé of Kristol, Michael Joyce, had been brought on as executive director. One of Joyce's contributions was to persuade the trustees to broaden the foundation's program to include the three "pillars" of a democratic capitalist system—the political institutions, the religious/cultural system and the economic system—a concept that had been put forward earlier by Kristol. Thereafter, the program became a model of focus and clarity.

In that same period William Simon, who had been secretary of the treasury under Nixon and was an old friend of Olin, was brought on the foundation's board. In 1982, when the donor died, Simon became his handpicked successor.

During the 1980s the Olin Foundation's resources, which had been rather modest, increased to some $75 million, and its grant level rose dramatically as a result. The pattern its grants have since taken clearly reflects the Kristol strategy of political transformation. The basic effort is intellectual, and the Olin Foundation has now implanted or reinforced centers of conservative thinking and research in leading colleges and universities throughout the country. In a few cases, such as the long-established Hoover Institution at Stanford University, general support has been offered. But in most cases the chair and its occupant, or the research project and its purposes, have been specifically funded. The recipient university's discretion has been limited to accepting or rejecting the targeted money. In addition to reaching influential professors, many Olin Foundation grants include research fellowships for younger faculty members and graduate students in order to reach the coming generation of policy thinkers.

Recognizing the crucial role of the media in influencing the political climate, the Olin Foundation has also supported leading conservative publications such as *The Public Interest;* William Buckley's program, "Firing Line," on public television; conservative student publications on campuses across the country; and conferences and seminars of many kinds, especially those rebroadcast on C-Span.

A third major focus, in recognition of the impact of government on the issues of greatest interest to the foundation, has been to distribute a large number of substantial Olin grants to research and public policy institutes in and around Washington, D.C.—the American Enterprise Institute, the Cato Institute, the Center for Strategic and International Studies, and the George Mason University School of Law, to name a few. Such centers have the advantage of ready access to government; they can draw on the talents and inside knowledge of individuals recently in high government posts, and their reports and policy recommendations attract great media attention. In addition, some of them, such as the Heritage Foundation, have played an important role in proposing the names of favored individuals for appointment to policy positions both in the executive branch and on congressional committee staffs.

Most recently, the Olin Foundation has extended its efforts to influence government policies to the state level, providing seed money to help launch think tanks in some thirty state capitals. The intent is to win over state legislators and local officials to the conservative agenda.

Not only has this foundation's strategic and tactical plan been sophisticated and comprehensive, but its selection of grantees has reflected a keen eye for talent and influence. Its list of individual beneficiaries reads like a *Who's Who* of the American right: Kristol in public policy, Robert Bork in law, Allan Bloom in education, Samuel Huntington in military affairs, Jeanne Kirkpatrick in international relations, and Herbert Stein and Milton Friedman in economics.

But not all of the foundation's grants have been triumphs, and some of them are even difficult to reconcile with its high-sounding purposes. For example, a campus newspaper the foundation has subsidized with nearly $300,000 in grants, *The Dartmouth Review,* in its first year sponsored a lobster-and-champagne feast to coincide with the campus fast for the world's hungry. Its former editor (still an Olin grantee) has been quoted as believing "the question is not whether women should be educated at Dartmouth but whether they should be educated at all." Later, on Yom Kippur, the most solemn Jewish holy day of the year, the paper carried an anti-Semitic quotation from Hitler on its masthead.

To some observers, grants to projects such as *The Dartmouth Review* suggested that the Olin Foundation was falling back into the old patterns of bigotry, social hostility, and irresponsibility that have defaced so many pro–free enterprise and anti-Communist philanthropic efforts in the past. Most such efforts, until quite recently, had been amateurish, episodic, and inconsequential.

Nevertheless, despite a few stumbles, John Olin's foundation has remained a powerful and focused voice in the national social, economic, and political dialogue. Though many may disagree with his social and political outlook, Olin was until his death in 1982 one of the most effective and influential philanthropists in recent times. He remains noteworthy for the clarity of his mission, his determination to make a major impact on national attitudes and policies, and his foundation's generally skillful pursuit of its objective. Since his death, his designated successor, William Simon, as chairman of his foundation's board, has continued to drive it in the same ideological direction.

Following the more recent death of John Olin's wife, the funds of the foundation have been augmented by her bequest. This will enable it to sustain its aggressive program for another ten or fifteen years, after which it will be closed down.

Chapter Fifteen

—❦—

Leveraging

The idea of leveraging one's gifts to charity, to multiply their impact by attracting other contributions, is old and familiar. Many donors—individuals, foundations, and government grant-making agencies—have used the method. Since several different kinds of leveraging can be used, it is useful to distinguish among them.

Historically, there have been some monumental examples of what might be called fortuitous leveraging. John Harvard in 1638 bequeathed his library of four hundred volumes plus £375 to a newly authorized college in the Massachusetts Bay Colony, and the institution was thereupon named after him. Today that institution is one of the world's preeminent universities with an endowment of some $5 billion.

In the latter half of the nineteenth century Leland Stanford—

railroad magnate, governor, and later senator—became the First Citizen of California. In 1884, at the height of Stanford's wealth and influence, his son and only child died at the age of sixteen. Devastated, Senator Stanford and his wife transmuted their grief into a plan to establish a new university in their son's name. This they did in 1885 with an initial endowment of $5 million. Now Stanford University in Palo Alto, it has become the West Coast counterpart of Harvard in prestige and in wealth, with an endowment in excess of $2 billion.

In 1829 an Englishman named James Smithson, who had never set foot in the United States, left eleven bags of gold sovereigns, then worth some $500,000, to create the Institution that bears his name in Washington, D. C., "for the increase and diffusion of new knowledge among men." It took more than ten years of wrangling in Congress before the gift was accepted, but today the Smithsonian Institution is a vast assemblage of fifteen major museums and nine major research centers, parks, and other facilities that receives an annual allotment from the federal government of more than $300 million plus an equal amount from research contracts and private gifts.

There is no evidence that any of these donors foresaw the formidable growth in population and wealth of the United States, its huge commitment to higher education, and the central role that the nation's capital would come to play in its cultural and scientific life—all of which explosively and fortuitously leveraged their gifts.

There is, however, a second kind of leverage in giving that can be planned for and specified. This is made up of matching gifts and challenge grants—donations that require the recipient to raise additional funds from other sources in order to obtain the original gift. The burden placed on the recipient can be fixed at a one-to-one, two-to-one, or any other ratio. Such matching requirements are now rather common practice by private donors and foundations, and by government agencies such as the National Endowment for the Arts. They can be helpful to the recipient organizations in giving them some leverage in their search for donations, but they can sometimes be exhausting, diversionary, or even destructive if the matching requirement is excessive or if the would-be recipient simply does not have the necessary fund-raising capacity. So donors resorting to this device should employ it selectively.

A third kind of leverage in grant making is what might be called "strategic." It involves the imposition of matching requirements for certain grants that are designed not simply to generate additional funds for a given project but also to achieve other important purposes. Andrew Carnegie in his public-library grants and Julius Rosenwald in his southern schoolhouse grants are good examples. In requiring matching contributions from local communities and commitments for ongoing operating support for the library buildings he funded, Carnegie wanted the citizenry to become involved, to take ownership of and responsibility for using and maintaining the new facilities. Likewise, Rosenwald, by imposing matching contribution requirements for his gifts for schoolhouses, hoped to generate a sense of community responsibility and a growth of community support for the idea of publicly supported schools, theretofore almost unknown in the postbellum South. These were powerful new philanthropic ideas in their time, and they worked.

Carnegie invented, perhaps inadvertently, an even more powerful kind of entrepreneurial leverage in his creation of the Teachers Insurance and Annuity Association—the now nationally known TIAA. At the start, in 1914, his intention was simply to pay for pensions for retiring teachers, but it soon became apparent that the cost of this would be far in excess of even his resources. Consequently, the program was reformulated to create a new kind of contributory pension and retirement insurance for teachers. The nonprofit insurance company that resulted is now the fifth largest insurance company and the largest pension fund in the United States, with 1,400,000 participants and total assets of $100 billion. Currently paying benefits to 230,000 retirees, it is self-sustaining.

The TIAA has been a very creative factor in the development of better and more flexible pension plans for all Americans, not only teachers and employees of nonprofit institutions. It is an example of "leverage" on a scale comparable only to the creation of Harvard and the Smithsonian, and it is a dramatic demonstration of the power of a timely and relevant idea. What is so extraordinary about this case is, first, Carnegie's action in creating it and, second, the rarity with which other great American business entrepreneurs have managed (or even tried) to do something equally creative in the nonprofit field.

There are two other interesting and important varieties of philanthropic leverage: the leveraging of public funds with private gifts, and "fecund" grants that generate spontaneous replications of themselves on a large scale.

Illustrative of the first variety is the work of Mary Lasker and her foundation in stimulating huge government-supported programs of medical research and health care. Irving Harris of Chicago, a donor with a long and distinguished career in philanthropy, has also effectively leveraged state and local government funding in support of his efforts to assist children and poor families in the housing projects of that city. Other examples of this kind of leverage are the initiatives of the Carnegie Corporation in the 1960s, which led to the creation of the Corporation for Public Broadcasting; the Ford Foundation grants that stimulated the development of various government programs in the War on Poverty in the 1960s and 1970s; and the agricultural research efforts of the Rockefeller Foundation, which have for many years stimulated greater governmental efforts and intergovernmental activity in this field. The role of foundations in accomplishing this sort of leverage is often exaggerated by both their admirers and their critics, but there have been a number of impressive and incontestable examples.

The next variety of leveraging results from the dramatic timeliness and attractiveness of certain philanthropic projects, their sheer fecundity in producing offspring. This is exemplified in recent times by the "I Have a Dream" program initiated by Eugene Lang, a successful New York businessman. It began almost inadvertently. Lang, a son of poor immigrant parents, attended public high school in New York City. Many years later, in June 1981, he was invited as a prominent alumnus to address the school's student body. As he stood before an audience made up largely of young blacks and Hispanics, he had the sudden impulse to offer all of them full college scholarship grants—if they would stay in school and complete their studies.

His offer stirred great excitement among the students and their parents, and it attracted much local and then national publicity. It came at a time when there was growing national concern about school dropouts and the spread of crime, drugs, and hopelessness in urban ghettos. Lang's offer seemed to strike directly at the roots of these problems, and he became an instant national hero. His "I Have a Dream" idea spread like wildfire among the many new American millionaires during the 1980s. Since then 157 such projects have been sponsored and funded by other rich men and women in cities throughout the country. Some twelve thousand "dreamers" have gone to college as a result.

As with the other kinds of fortuitous leveraging described earlier, this kind of multiplication or leverage cannot be planned for, or hardly even hoped for. Nonetheless it shows that a sufficiently dramatic and timely spark can sometimes produce a beautiful bonfire.

There remains perhaps the most pertinent and feasible philanthropic leverage that almost all serious donors may employ in their efforts to maximize the benefits and the impact of their gifts of funds, *namely, to give or invest themselves—their time, talents, experience, and energy—along with their money.*

Three instructive recent examples of such leverage are the cases of Frederick P. Rose and New York's Lincoln Center for the Performing Arts, James D. Wolfensohn and New York's venerable Carnegie Hall, and Lee Iacocca and his leadership of the monumental—and highly controversial—national fund-raising campaign to restore the Statue of Liberty and Ellis Island as national monuments.

Frederick P. Rose

Frederick P. Rose is a highly successful East Coast real-estate developer. He has carried on an equally successful career as a philanthropist and civic worker. In earlier years he was prominent in both Jewish and nonsectarian charitable work. He has been a generous supporter of higher education and has been a board member of several prestigious institutions, including Yale University, the Metropolitan Museum of Art, and Lincoln Center, New York City's premier cultural complex.

Rose is an active worker on every board on which he sits. His leadership of a recent major project for Lincoln Center is a good example of how donors can leverage the ultimate benefits of a gift by contributing their experience and business skills along with their money.

Lincoln Center, which includes an opera house, ballet hall, theater, music school, film center, and other elements, had by the early 1980s grown to the point where it urgently needed additional facilities for rehearsal and screening space, dormitories, administrative offices, and other purposes. Given the center's location in an intensively developed area of New York City, the obstacles and costs of adding a new complex of mixed-use buildings were enormous. There were zoning problems, problems of acquiring from the city an adjacent obsolete public high school on the site where the new buildings would have to stand, problems of negotiating the sale of "air rights"—an intangible asset of great potential value in the New York setting—and problems of opposition from the local community.

Rose volunteered his services to perform all the roles that a "developer" would perform in such a situation. He selected, assembled, and coordinated the team of experts required—lawyers, community relations experts, specialized real-estate consultants, architects, engineers, and others. He played an important role in shaping the concept of the new complex so that it would meet the various needs of the different elements of the center. By including a residential apartment structure, he planned to provide the center with a major capital gain—or, if the building were not sold, with a continuing flow of income as a rental property.

Rose personally guided the execution of the total plan so that the architecture would be harmonious with the existing structures. Later he negotiated the sale of the air rights over the center's new facilities, which added some $50 million to its general endowment. At the same time he played a major part in an additional and successful $100 million fund-raising effort for the new project.

In effect Rose put many months of sweat equity into the undertaking. Moreover, when the fund-raising effort was well along and when the many basic obstacles to the new building program had been cleared away, he climaxed his multiple contributions by joining with his wife in making an anonymous personal contribution of $15 million to permit completion of the Lincoln Center addition. All told, the total benefits to Lincoln Center of Rose's efforts were a new $150 million complex. Simply in dollar terms, he had leveraged his family's gift by a factor of ten. The multiplier in the equation was that he gave so much of himself and his abilities in addition to his money.

But the additional and incalculable benefits to the center were the quality of the end product, both functionally and aesthetically, and the relative speed with which the project was accomplished (it might easily have been mired in litigation and negotiation for several years). Most incalculable of all is the question of whether the project could ever have been accomplished at all without the special skills and experience that Rose was able to bring to bear.

Now, with the Lincoln Center project accomplished, Rose has made a new commitment to an equally large and complex undertaking to plan and construct a major addition to the great Museum of Natural History in New York.

James Wolfensohn

James Wolfensohn is another donor who has powerfully leveraged his gifts by his personal involvement in two major philanthropic projects. An investment banker, he led a major effort in the 1980s to refurbish the famous Carnegie Hall in New York. He then took the leadership in a large-scale rescue and rejuvenation campaign in behalf of Kennedy Center in Washington D.C.

Born in Australia in a family of modest means, Wolfensohn has had a rapid rise as an investment banker, first in London and then in the United States. The partners in his prestigious New York firm have included such luminaries as Paul Volcker, former chairman of the Federal Reserve Board, and Harold Brown, once head of the California Institute of Technology, and later U.S. secretary of defense.

Paralelling his business activities, Wolfensohn from the beginning has had a strong interest in cultural, philanthropic, and intellectual matters. He has been a trustee of the Rockefeller Foundation and has chaired the board of the Institute for Advanced Studies at Princeton. He and his wife have their own foundation, and his banking firm has given a stunning 20 percent of its profits each year to charity.

Wolfensohn's personal passion is music. He has played the piano since childhood, and his daughter is now an aspiring concert pianist. Musicians like Isaac Stern, Mstislav Rostropovich, and Yo Yo Ma are among his closest friends. In 1977 he began to take cello lessons from the cellist Jacqueline du Pré to help convince her that she could teach even after multiple sclerosis had destroyed her ability to perform on the instrument. He learned enough to celebrate his fiftieth birthday by playing in a string quartet in Carnegie Hall with Isaac Stern as first violinist.

These multiple talents, along with his warm personality, have made Wolfensohn a man with a virtually unique status in business and in cultural and intellectual circles. And the combination of his strong interests and special status have enabled him greatly to multiply the impact of his own contributions to the cultural institutions with which he has been associated. The first major example was his leadership of the campaign to save the venerable Carnegie Hall in New York from the wrecker's ball in the 1980s.

Tonally perfect and beloved by musicians the world over, the concert hall had been a financial disaster from the beginning, rarely turning a profit in its entire ninety-year life. It had become shabby and decaying as a result, and the initial estimates were that at least $30 million would be required for its rehabilitation, a sum far greater than the board felt any fund-raising effort could produce. There was serious consideration given, therefore, to its demolition.

Nevertheless, Wolfensohn took on the task of trying to save it. He began by overhauling the chaotic concert schedule and Carnegie Hall's antiquated promotional policies as well, drawing on the advice of his friends in the world of music as well as on his own business experience.

To get the fund-raising started, Wolfensohn made a $1 million contribution of his own and recruited a group of the most eminent names in New York's financial and cultural circles to join the effort. Together they were able to generate a total of $80 million in capital gifts and pledges. The list of regular annual contributors was also increased from fewer than eight hundred to more then nine thousand, and for the first time the hall is operating in the black.

Wolfensohn's term as chairman ended in 1990, at which point the hall had been completely renovated and a capital reserve had been accumulated. It had not only been saved but greatly strengthened in its management as well as its finances. And Jim Wolfensohn, by combining his business talents, his prestige with the New York business and cultural establishment, and a great deal of hard work, in effect leveraged his own direct gift to the project by a factor of eighty or more.

That unlikely triumph having been achieved, Wolfensohn then agreed to become chairman of the Kennedy Center in Washington-D.C., arguably the worst-run concert hall in the country. It needed

$45 million to renovate its run-down facade and six stages, and it was operating deep in the red. Wolfensohn was prudent enough to line up promises of support from Congress and the White House before committing himself, but once committed, he began promptly to clean up the mess, starting by upgrading the program schedule. Benefiting from his experience on the board of the Columbia Broadcasting System, he then proposed to give the Kennedy Center a "seventh stage" by beaming concerts onto millions of American television sets. After that would come the problem of generating sustained local support for the center from a community that has never been keen on the complex.

Whether he might have been able to work his magic a second time in the rehabilitation of a major cultural center will now not be known because in early 1995 he was named head of the World Bank, a full-time job even for this immensely energetic man.

Lee Iacocca

Lee Iacocca's campaign to restore the Statue of Liberty in New York Harbor in time for the 1986 centennial celebration of its dedication is another example of the leveraging effect of donor involvement.

Maintenance and upkeep of the monument had been neglected for years. The same was true of the old immigration center on nearby Ellis Island. In earlier years various ideas for raising private funds to restore them had been put forth, but nothing had happened. So in 1982 the Reagan administration appointed a blue-ribbon citizens commission to organize a nationwide effort. A vast multimedia campaign to solicit contributions was envisaged, and prominent figures were asked successively to head it, all of whom declined. Finally Lee Iacocca, head of the Chrysler Motor Company and a son of Italian immigrants, agreed to take on the labor.

By his success in saving that desperately troubled automobile company a few years earlier, and by his frequent appearances on television and his best-selling autobiography, he had become a kind of folk hero at the time.

Once Iacocca had accepted the job, he threw himself into it with gusto and flair. "I don't just write checks," he said, "I drive." He made himself the sole television spokesman for the effort, and he became its chief fund-raiser. After the estimated costs of the restorations had risen from some $50 million to nearly $200 million, Iacocca personally raised the goal of the campaign from $50 million to $230 million—"a dollar for every American" as he said.

Drawing on his experience in mass merchandising, Iacocca devised a strategy of first seeking major corporate sponsors. As in the fund-raising for the 1984 Olympics in Los Angeles, on which his plan was based, dozens of the largest and best-known companies were offered exclusive rights to use the Statue of Liberty image in their advertising in return for contributions to the campaign. As a result Miss Liberty and Ellis Island soon had their "official" newspaper, soft drink, wine, beer, cigarette, airline, and even bologna.

By 1986, the anniversary year of the statue, Iacocca announced that the campaign had raised some $170 million in cash and pledges. At that point he arranged with the U.S. Treasury to cover the shortfall of $50 million through the issuance and sale of commemorative coins.

In the end the campaign was not a clear and acclaimed triumph, partly because the government had to step in to help it reach its goals, and partly because of widespread criticism that Iacocca had demeaned the monuments by commercializing them and by his own egocentric behavior.

Nonetheless, this man took on a task others had declined, he used techniques of merchandising familiar to him through his business experience, and he labored hard to try to make the effort a success. It is not known whether he personally made any significant cash contribution to the campaign, but in purely dollar terms he leveraged his efforts for a public purpose many times over.

Chapter Sixteen

—ⴰⴱⵣⴱⵖ—

Capital Gifts, Deals, and Deal Making

If foundations are the most over-recognized and over-rated form of philanthropy, capital gifts are the most under-recognized and under-rated. Conventional wisdom among foundation professionals holds that setting up a foundation is a sophisticated and creative form of philanthropy while making capital gifts is passive and banal.

But from the perspective of donors the choice may be seen very differently. Foundation launching can be laborious and risky while the making of capital gifts appears to be a simple and secure kind of investment. In the former there are all the speculative uncertainties of a new venture, while in the latter one is dealing with a respected and established institution that stands on its record. The long, long list of capital gifts made each year by American donors—

including small, midsize, and large—is the most conclusive evidence of how well this type of gift, with its many variations, fits their varied interests and circumstances.

Perhaps the central misunderstanding of nondonors relates to the creative, initiative-taking aspects of gift making. There are donors who simply out of loyalty or love for an institution make unrequited gifts to it. But in a great many instances large gift making is a process of transactions in which quid pro quos are exchanged, the calculations being in the peculiar coin of the nonprofit world: the donor's name on a building, an honorary degree, an agreement to carry out a particular program of research or teaching. The donor's "profit" is taken in the form of public recognition, prestige, remembrance, or the agreement of the university or hospital to establish, for example, a named professorship, research institute, or nursery for premature babies.

In some cases the transactions are money for money—gifts with a requirement that matching funds be raised from other sources, for example. But in most cases they represent an exchange of funds for an intangible. Since significant amounts of money are involved, there are negotiations to be conducted (simple or complex, brief or extended) and, in the end, deals to be struck.

Because many donors have had long business experience and can be tough traders, the record is full of protracted and sometimes highly contentious proceedings. Given the great variety of donor demands and tactics, it is not possible to define the rules of this peculiar market neatly. But at least one principle does seem to operate, namely, the larger the sum of money, the greater the concessions made by the grantee and the more elaborate and intricate the agreements that are reached.

This chapter first offers a sketch of the prevailing "prices" of various concessions that museums, universities, hospitals, or other such institutions are prepared to offer donors for smaller or larger gifts. These are simply indicative of what donors can reasonably ask for in return for their gift.

Second, it will describe the elements of a large and complex arrangement that one educational institution, the Massachusetts Institute of Technology, recently made with a big donor, which illustrates some of the kinds of issues that tend to arise.

Third, it will describe the long-standing war between Stanford University and the Hoover Institution, sustained by the latter's fund-raising capabilites.

Fourth, it will analyze the much-publicized case of the Hirshhorn Museum, which involved a major private gift to an agency of the U.S. government, with all the institutional, political and fortuitous factors that entered into the prolonged and ultimately successful negotiations.

Fifth, it will describe Walter Annenberg's skillful means of balancing control over and respect for the institutions that have received his large gifts.

And sixth, it will tell the cautionary tale of Armand Hammer, an irresponsible donor whose unremitting connivance and excessive demands exceeded the acceptable limits and ultimately brought him only failure and disgrace.

"Prices" in the Market for Capital Gifts

In making a modest capital gift to a church, college, museum, hospital, or other operating nonprofit institutions, the donor or his/her foundation has the choice of simply contributing to its fund-raising campaign, the quid pro quo of which may be simply to have one's name listed and published in an honorific category such as "donor," "patron," or "benefactor," determined by the amount given.

For somewhat larger gifts there is a huge supermarket of "memorial" offerings," each of which carries a price tag. As in every kind of market, there are those obscure and local institutions whose prices are modest, and there are those prestigious institutions where charges for various forms of public recognition of a donor can be extremely high.

There are churches where a pew can be named for a family for $500, and churches where that would cost a donor $5,000; libraries where a name on a children's reading room could cost $5,000, and others where it would cost $250,000; hospitals where a name on a premature babies nursery could cost anything from $50,000 to $250,000.

It is at the elite university level that the rules have been most elaborated and the prices most elevated. At one Ivy League school, the requirement for the naming of a building is that the donor must supply at least half the cost of the entire structure. The name will remain until the building is torn down, when its replacement would presumably bear the name of some new donor.

Programs that are supported with expendable money—the "Murphy Lectures"—bear the donor's name as long as the money lasts. When the support changes, the name changes: "the Murphy Lectures" become "the Hannigan Lectures." Names that are put on permanent endowment funds, however, remain forever—the Boesky Fund remains the Boesky Fund—although the name appears only in the records and in occasional published reports.

Increasingly, responding to the widespread desire of donors for some kind of formal and individual recognition, institutions have developed elaborate arrangements for what are now called "naming opportunities"—facilities, or parts of facilities, and programs that are identified with a particular donor or family.

Museums have probably carried the memorial device to its outer limits. Following are a few items from the unpublished gift-price list of one prominent urban museum:

Wing, including galleries	$10,000,000–25,000,000
Auditorium seats (each)	$10,000
Chief curator's office	$100,000
International exhibitions fund	$750,000
Public programs fund	$2,000,000
Visiting scholars fund	$750,000
Film series	$400,000
Lecture series	$350,000
Publications fund	$1,000,000
Main staircase	$1,500,000
Coat room	$250,000
Passenger elevator (each)	$250,000
Picture gallery	$1,000,000
Women's or men's toilet	$50,000

The prices of gifts such as the above may involve some limited negotiation, but they are rather firm, for the institutions have developed their prices after careful study of their "market" and of the level of prices of their closest competitors. For megagifts, however, the range and duration of negotiations can be very considerable.

A Megagift Transaction: The Whitehead Institute and MIT

In 1939 Edwin Whitehead and his father started the Technicon Corporation, which grew to be a major supplier of automated equipment for clinical laboratory analysis. The company was very profitable, and it was sold in the 1970s for some $400 million. Edwin Whitehead, the son, decided to put a good part of his wealth into philanthropy, and because it had come from advances in medical research, he decided to "return some of that wealth to its source."

Whitehead's first initiative, in 1974, was to underwrite a new biomedical institute at Duke University with a gift of $100 million. However, the deal fell through shortly afterwards over issues of management and the recruitment of key faculty. Whitehead gave Duke $10 million as a consolation present and remarked later that the experience had taught him that "it's easier to make $100 million than to give it away."

He then entered into discussions with the Massachusetts Institute of Technology and Harvard about the creation of a new joint health sciences and technology program. That also ran aground because of unbridgeable differences between the parties. Finally, Whitehead and MIT were able to agree on the creation of a new biomedical research institute that would not be a part of MIT's organizational structure but would share faculty, board memberships, and some facilities. Whitehead agreed to provide about $20 million to build a research laboratory for the new institute, to fund its activities at a level of $5 million a year until his death, and thereafter to convey to it an endowment of at least $100 million.

After several years of negotiations, the following agreements were reached, which were then carefully spelled out in legal documents:
 · The new research institute would have its own board; MIT would have only minority representation on it.
 · The institute's director would be appointed by its board, and with MIT's approval he would be made an MIT professor. The institute

would make a certain number of staff appointments who would also be given MIT faculty positions, and their salaries would be comparable to MIT salaries. Some of these appointments would be tenured, others not.

· Additional graduate students would be admitted by MIT because of the presence of the new professors.

· To help meet any unforeseen costs the university might have to bear because of the new institute, Whitehead would provide a $7.5 million special endowment.

· The original board would be made up of Edwin Whitehead's three children and eight other directors named by him, plus three named by MIT, and three others named jointly by the Board and MIT.

All these points of understanding required careful negotiation between MIT and Whitehead, who had extensive experience in high-tech business and with various scientific and technical organizations. He wanted to create a high-quality scientific institution as a personal and family memorial, to involve his family in its direction, and to link it with, but not subordinate it to, the university. The university had to balance the benefits it would gain from its association with a fully financed and semi-independent research institution (including the possibility of future income from patents that might result) against the risks involved in lending its name and prestige to an institute which it could not fully control (including the possibly negative impact that its various concessions might have on faculty sensibilities and university prerogatives). These countervailing considerations were ultimately balanced out, and agreement was reached.

A Nobel laureate was chosen to head the new institute, and high-quality scientists were recruited. The resulting research program is now well regarded in its field. Nevertheless, at times strains and frictions have developed and created serious problems, but these have been manageable because both parties to the original negotiations were knowledgeable, experienced, and kept their demands within reasonable bounds.

The case of the Whitehead Institute illustrates clearly, even vividly, the complexities that making major capital gifts may involve. Perhaps it also exemplifies the realistic limits of a happy outcome from the point of view of both donor and beneficiary.

Stanford University
and the Hoover Institution
on War, Revolution, and Peace

The association of the Hoover Institution with Stanford University represents the longest-running struggle on record between a donor and a recipient nonprofit institution. In the end, the struggle may prove to have been to the benefit of both.

Herbert Hoover, from his days as relief administrator in Europe during World War I, through his term as president of the United States, and thereafter, was an avid collector of documentary materials on the causes and consequences of wars. In 1919, when his collection of historical documents was already considerable, he offered a grant of $50,000 to his alma mater, Stanford University, to send a team of scholars to Europe to assist in gathering the historical records of the First World War. As tons of documents began to arrive at the school, Hoover made further grants to establish his war library "as a separate collection within the university library." The influx of materials continued. In 1920 the collection was assigned an entire wing of the university library, and its name was changed to the Hoover War Library. Hoover provided funds for acquisitions, but the university had to bear the costs of housing and administering them. Given the murky terms of his understanding with the university, many quarrels developed over money, control, and the separate identity of the collection.

By 1925 the continuing flood of documents had overwhelmed the university facilities, and a new building was needed. In this period the staff of the Hoover began to envision its future as a full-fledged research center with its own researchers, completely separate from the university. The university vetoed this idea, which contributed to further tension.

When Hoover returned from Washington in 1933, he took a vigorous hand in raising money from his friends and from a number of eastern foundations for a new tower library to be located on the Stanford campus. This was completed in 1941, and the ceremonies at its opening marked a momentary cordiality between Hoover and the university. Soon thereafter, as Hoover encouraged the development of the library's own staff and research operations, the long struggle with the university over separation and independence intensified. The issues expanded beyond matters of academic jealousy and turf into an ideological contest between academic liberals and library conservatives.

In 1946 a temporary settlement was reached making the library "a separate division of the University" under the control of an advisory board controlled by Hoover. But in 1949 the university faculty, denouncing Hoover as a "meddlesome reactionary," briefly reestablished university control.

Over the next twelve years the brutal conflict continued. The university faculty, enraged by the presence of what it regarded as an ideologically offensive group in its midst, kept pressing for control, while Hoover and a group of wealthy friends utilized their power over funding to fight back. By a sudden cutoff of their support for the university, the Hoover group provoked a financial crisis in 1957–58. This led to their decisive victory in 1959—a written agreement giving independence to the newly designated Hoover Institution on War, Revolution, and Peace, removing faculty oversight committees, and appointing a new director, Glenn Campbell, chosen by Hoover.

Immediately thereafter Hoover was able to attract a major infusion of funds from a group of conservative foundations and individuals, and in 1962 he won further and final concessions of freedom from university interference.

The former U.S. president died in 1964, having survived fifty years of dedicated service to and combat with his alma mater. Since then the Hoover Institution has achieved massive growth in its staff, publications, physical facilities, endowment, and national influence. With an endowment of more than $125 million and more than eighty research scholars, including several Nobelists and other eminent intellectuals, it can now claim to be the preeminent national and international research library for twentieth-century economic, political, and social affairs.

Without its totally engaged and determined donor, who had the singular prestige of a former president, the Hoover Institution could never have achieved that status. But present donors may reasonably ask if all that struggle was necessary just to be located in Palo Alto. Were there no less-obstructed paths that could have been taken? Or has the outcome been worth all the contest—having produced a highly stimulating intellectual tension on a single university campus between strong, competitive centers of liberal and conservative thought? If the latter is an objective assessment, the benefits to scholarship and education may have been worth far more than the costs, and the outcome should be considered a major success.

Joseph Hirshhorn:
All-Time Big Winner

Joseph H. Hirshhorn was born in Latvia in 1899, one of thirteen children. His widowed mother brought them all to the United States when the boy was only six and supported the family by working in a purse factory.

Little Joey quit school at thirteen to go to work as a newsboy. By the time he was sixteen he had become a stock trader on Wall Street. Before he was thirty he had made, lost, and remade several fortunes. Having splendidly survived the great stock market crash of 1929, he then began to look for new opportunities to apply his talents as a trader and speculator. That took him to Canada, where within a few years he had built a small empire of gold mines. But his great coup was to come following World War II, when the advent of atomic energy and the acquisition of nuclear weapons by the Soviet Union had made uranium the ore of the future.

Taking a gamble based on the hunch of a geologist he had encountered, Hirshhorn was able to locate the prime area of uranium reserves in Canada. He then beat the competition by secretly staking out thousands of mining claims and afterwards rapidly developing his mining operations. By the mid-1950s Hirshhorn mines were producing more uranium than all 625 of the mines then operating in the United States, and he had hundreds of millions of dollars in government contracts.

At that point the major mining organizations in the world were eager to buy Hirshhorn out. By playing one against another, he was able in the end to get nearly $100 million for his interests from the Rothschilds' Rio Tinto company, then headed by Great Britain's earl of Bessborough. The moment the formal documents were signed, Hirshhorn, unable to contain his excitement, ran down the hall with his lawyer to the men's room. After peeping under the booths to make sure they were alone, he executed a gleeful buck-and-wing and burst into laughter. "Imagine me!" he chortled. "The little Hebe from Latvia making this deal with the Royal House of England!"

Hirshhorn was a tangle of contradictions. A smoker of thirty cigars a day, he was a man of ferocious energy. His manners were rough, and his business methods even rougher. Yet he was ebullient, funny, and unpretentious.

In business he was endlessly successful, with an entrepreneur's vision and a gambler's nerve. But his personal life was a shambles, with a succession of divorces and terrible relations with his children. He was compulsively acquisitive about money—and strangely enough, also about art. Indeed, collecting art, along with getting rich, had long been a passion with him. To it he brought all his talents of self-confidence, energy, vision, and willingness to gamble on his judgment, and his appetite for art was as unslakable as his appetite for wealth. He did his own legwork—studying, roaming the galleries and auctions, and visiting artists in their studios. The sheer quantity of his acquisitions was prodigious. He began collecting in the late 1920s, and by the 1930s he was buying some 60 works a year; by the 1940s, 150; by the 1950s, more than 200, and by the 1960s (after his uranium coup), more than 700. In all during his lifetime he assembled a collection of more than 12,000 works, including paintings and sculptures.

Almost from the start, Hirshhorn's commitment was to contemporary art, and primarily to the work of young American artists. By the 1950s portions of his holdings were being exhibited by prestigious museums at home and abroad, and leading art authorities were calling the Hirshhorn collection "the most important and comprehensive" of its kind in the world.

Sometime around 1960 he began to think that he wanted his own museum to house the immense array of objects—and at about that same time important museums in various countries, including the United States, began to think about the possibilities of creating a major new museum of contemporary art. Once again, as in the case of uranium, a favorable configuration of circumstances began to open up bright trading possibilities for Hirshhorn. Museums in Canada, Israel, Switzerland, and elsewhere began to approach him with proposals. For a time he seriously considered an offer from Florence, but when he learned he would have to pay the Italian government a 15 percent tax on the value of his gift, he dropped that possibility. Next he seriously considered an offer from Her Majesty Queen Elizabeth of several acres of land in London's Regent's Park plus the construction of an appropriate building to house the collection.

The queen's offer was eclipsed by a proposal from S. Dillon Ripley, an aristocratic and scholarly New Englander who was head of the Smithsonian Institution in Washington. Ripley happened to discover a provision in an old law authorizing the U.S. president to assign a site on the Capitol Mall for a museum of contemporary art as a counterpart to the National Gallery and its Old Masters. Ripley decided the time had come—indeed the hour was late—to create that museum. And the best way to make up for lost time was to find someone who had already created the needed collection. An ornithologist by training, Ripley pounced like a hawk on the possibility of capturing Hirshhorn and his collection.

In mid-1964 Ripley wrote Hirshhorn a tantalizing letter saying that the Smithsonian had "a lively interest in establishing the

American equivalent of the Tate Gallery in London" and suggest-
ing they get together "to explore the concept." The initial steps in
the courtship were taken, and early the following year Hirshhorn's
lawyer, Sam Harris, a man wise in the ways of the world and of
Washington, went to visit Ripley. Although the discussion was a
preliminary one, Harris came prepared to put forward Hirshhorn's
two basic demands. When Ripley at one point carefully inquired
whether Hirshhorn might consider giving his collection to the
Smithsonian, Harris replied, "He would want his name on the museum." When Ripley said that would be no problem, Harris went a
large step further. "On the Mall?" he asked. "I don't see why not,"
replied Ripley. Suppressing his astonishment, Harris said, "You
mean, a Hirshhorn Museum on the Mall?"

Recognizing that the question really had to do with the matter
of anti-Semitism, Ripley replied, "This is 1965. I think America has
grown up." Ripley had definitely gotten Hirshhorn's attention with
that exchange, but there was much more to do. In a follow-up letter he stressed that the collection would retain its independent
identity within the Smithsonian Institution and that it would be
seen by millions of people annually. At the same time he called for
reinforcements in the form of Lady Bird Johnson and the president
himself. Mrs. Johnson visited Hirshhorn's Connecticut estate twice
to see some of his works and charmed him completely.

Finally all the panoply of the White House was employed—a
formal reception and private tour for the Hirshhorns, followed by
a luncheon with various cultural eminences and power brokers, at
the end of which the president left a Cabinet meeting to join them.
At the crucial moment the six-foot-plus President put his bearlike
hug on the five-foot-plus visitor and said, "Joe, you don't need a
contract. Just turn the collection over to the Smithsonian and I'll

take care of the rest." Hirshhorn almost succumbed on the spot. "Once the president puts his arm around your shoulder," he said later, "you're a dead cookie."

But Hirshhorn's attorney was not a dead cookie. Harris told the president's advisor, Abe Fortas (later to be a Supreme Court justice), "Over my dead body are you going to get this collection without the conditions written into a contract and a statute passed." In the discussions that followed, Hirshhorn secured formal assurances that his name would be on a new museum on the Mall and that he would not have to turn over his collection until the new structure was standing.

The Smithsonian in turn got its crucial demand, namely that the trustees of the museum would have the power to sell or exchange items from the collection in the future. There is reason to believe that its insistence on this point reflected a strong view among art professionals that the Hirshhorn collection, though strong, represented essentially the tastes and times of one man and that modern art was too vast and dynamic to be confined by that. For the Smithsonian this concern was sharpened by its experience with the dead hand of the donor on its Freer Gallery of Oriental art, a splendid but now stagnant institution.

After these basic agreements were reached, the gift was formally made in May 1966. Ground was broken three years later, on a cold January day in 1969, with Hirshhorn standing in his mink coat between the nation's huge president and the even taller Ripley. Not one to be stifled by solemnity, he began his speech by saying, "They should have given me a high chair." He then went on to speak movingly of the early poverty of his immigrant family and of his lifelong confidence that "the explosive energy of American art would one day affect art all over the world." The art critic of the *Washing-*

ton Post wrote about him: "Standing on a box so he could see over the podium, the bow tie and the mink coat both made sense. There was poverty mixed with money in his voice."

It took another six years before the tortuous processes of legislation, design, and construction were completed. During that long period it became evident that additional concessions had been accorded Hirshhorn. He had been given a virtual veto over the general design of the building. For example, when initially the architect presented plans for a museum that would be largely underground, Hirshhorn was outraged. "You're not going to bury me in a bomb shelter," he snapped. "You can bury yourself." That plan was scrapped. The museum's board was to be independent of the Smithsonian and its bureaucracy, and Hirshhorn had secured the right to appoint half its members with himself as chairman. He also secured the appointment of the man he had hired as curator of his collection, Abram Lerner, as head of the new museum, even though Lerner lacked the usual academic credentials for such a post.

But controversy continued to swirl around every aspect of the project—especially the naming of the new structure, its architecture, its impact on the sweep of the Mall, and the costs. It was the expressed view of some senators and representatives that Hirshhorn was nothing more than "a petty criminal" unworthy to have his name graven alongside those of Washington, Lincoln, and Jefferson. One influential journalist denounced the whole transaction as a gigantic swindle: "The truth is, this isn't a gift, it's plain theft. . . . Art that cost Hirshhorn a maximum of $5 million will cost the taxpayers as much as $100 million ($20 million in construction costs plus $80 million in tax write-offs) plus a government obligation to pay $2 million a year forever to maintain the museum."

When all this became public, the art critic Aline Saarinen, a one-time admirer of Hirshhorn, wrote angrily, "Joe has taken the government as it's never been taken before."

But in the end, Ripley's masterful diplomacy and the heavy influence of the White House prevailed. The museum now stands on the Mall, a familiar and accepted part of the Washington scene. The controversies have died down, and its prestige has grown steadily as the trustees have carried out a vigorous and discriminating program of selling and trading some of the original pieces to upgrade and update the collection.

For Hirshhorn the whole affair was a long, rough ride, but because he had a good sense of what he wanted most (his name on a national monument) and was willing to compromise on the Smithsonian's key demand (that the museum board have discretion in developing the collection), the result is a museum that can continue indefinitely to be a living, evolving, high-quality institution for the presentation of contemporary art, funded by the American government in perpetuity. The stars had to be in their right configuration to have made this extraordinary outcome possible— Hirshhorn was lucky as well as prudent and purposeful—and the success he ultimately achieved was almost beyond even the most ambitious donor's dreams.

Walter Annenberg's Deal-Making Machine

Walter Annenberg has long been a skillful and sophisticated philanthropist. He has been generous and creative, and he has also believed in focusing his grants on clearly defined objectives and maintaining considerable control over the use of his funds. This has brought him to the edge of invading the jurisdiction and integrity of his grantees, but by his own self-imposed restraint, he has eased, if not dispelled, their fears, that he might transgress the boundary line. In this respect his approach to grant making probably defines the degree of control over grantees that a donor can reasonably claim.

Among Annenberg's creative acts as a donor, one of the most useful for his style and purposes was the nonprofit educational corporation he established in the late 1950s called the Annenberg School of Communications, based in Radnor, Pennsylvania. He generously endowed it with nearly one-third of the shares in his Triangle company, a gift with a value on the order of $1 billion. Its legal status as a school offered many tax and other advantages to the donor. One of these was that as a school, technically defined as a nonprofit charity by the Internal Revenue Service, the Annenberg School could make grants to other institutions on the condition that their purpose was consistent with its goals and that it helped operate the programs it funded.

The Annenberg School in Radnor, which had no faculty, classrooms, or students of its own, therefore worked out "operating agreements" with several leading universities (including the University of Pennsylvania, Northwestern, and the University of Southern California) for the creation of jointly directed Annenberg Schools of Communications. In each instance, a joint board of trustees was created, half appointed by the host university and half by the Annenberg School at Radnor. These operating agreements ran usually for ten-year periods. The Radnor school provided the funds, and the university carried out the program. In effect, Annenberg, building on the established reputation of the universities, subcontracted out his programs, specifying the terms and purposes, sharing in their ongoing overall control, and keeping them on a relatively short financial leash by way of renewable term grants. Annenberg's huge grant of $150 million to the Public Broadcasting Corporation was also made through the Annenberg School in Radnor and governed by a joint board in Annenberg's usual pattern. The Radnor school could therefore be seen as the control center of a kind of nonprofit conglomerate as well as a sophisticated philanthropic deal-making machine.

Needless to say, reactions by university people have been very diverse. Some were coldly pragmatic. The head of one of the Annenberg projects said, "The fact of the matter is that no gift comes without strings. If you pay the bill, you should be able to call the tune. If you don't want the money, you don't have to accept it. It's as simple as that." The head of another said, "It's a trade-off. You give away a lot of authority. But you get a lot out of it." An officer of the American Council of Education called the ten-year contract arrangement "very clever and reasonably appropriate."

But Clark Kerr, a prominent educator and onetime head of the University of California at Berkeley, said he would never have recommended such an arrangement to his board of regents: "I think a lot of people would be troubled sharing control with a single powerful outsider."

The first head of the Annenberg School at the University of Pennsylvania was the distinguished critic Gilbert Seldes. He had no previous university experience and was uneasy about the role Annenberg had been allowed to play. "It is my abiding conviction," he wrote in 1964, "that no one connected with Walter Annenberg— nor himself—has ever done anything improper by his own standards. . . . They believe the School is theirs and remains theirs so long as they put up the money. . . . They haven't heard of independence of mind, they know that academic freedom is something some crackpot and probably subversive professors talk about.

They have made an investment—they have associated with themselves the prestige of a university—and they expect the investment to pay off."

But Seldes's successor, George Gerbner, later said about the arrangement, "It's a miracle it works. If there was ever a disagreement on the school's purposes or goals it could create a lot of trouble. Fortunately Ambassador Annenberg has never tried to enforce his academic opinions."

This history of mixed reactions to Annenberg's use of the Radnor school to exert control over his grantees provides a clear reminder of the sensitivity of universities to intrusions on their turf. It also gives testimony to the fine line Annenberg was able to walk between the rights and responsibilities of a donor and his grantees.

Now that he has in effect dismantled this control device by converting the Radnor school into a foundation as part of the final restructuring of his philanthropy, the case is just a part of history. But it is an instructive part.

Armand Hammer: An Instance of Compulsive Excess

Deal making can be an amusement for some donors, or a way of life, or in some cases a sickness. Perhaps the most instructive example of the latter is the case of Armand Hammer, the late California oilman and art collector, who carried philanthropic deal making to a point where it was destructive to the potential beneficiaries, to his company, and ultimately to his own reputation.

Hammer had a variety of business interests in the course of his career, but his principal achievement was the building of the Occidental Oil Company of Los Angeles. He also had a longtime interest in art, dating from the years after World War I when he accepted a collection of expropriated oil paintings as payment for a transaction with the struggling young Soviet Union. That started him in art dealing and art collecting, an important sideline to his activities as an oilman for the rest of his life.

In the period of the Cold War, as his oil company grew, Hammer carefully cultivated his reputation as an American businessman who had good relations with the Kremlin, and he periodically announced grandiose joint projects with the Soviet Union, most of which subsequently evaporated. In parallel, he was frequently in the newspapers with announcements of major promised gifts of art to various museums. The Los Angeles County Museum of Art was a particular focus of these initiatives. In 1975 a large collection of prints by the French satirist Daumier was offered for sale to the museum by the owner, but the museum stepped aside when Dr. Hammer said he would buy it and bequeath it to the museum. A few years later the museum held back from bidding on a group of late-nineteenth-century French paintings, a weakness in its collections, in deference to Hammer, who had indicated his intention to acquire and give them to the museum. In both cases he got the paintings—but the museum never did. Over the period from 1975 to 1985 Hammer repeatedly arranged for the museum to show portions of his collection in conjunction with social functions he wanted. On these occasions he would typically get some publicity by underscoring his intention eventually to make a gift of his collection to the museum.

The president of the museum board, of which Hammer was a member, has said that their assumption was that in addition to the collection Hammer intended to leave the museum a substantial fund for future acquisitions. This happy atmosphere of courtship and expectation turned to bitterness in 1988 when Hammer announced plans to build his own museum in Los Angeles to house his collection, including the pictures he had promised repeatedly to give to the County Museum. This brought down an avalanche of criticism from leading citizens of the city.

When Hammer's museum opened in late 1990, a new storm broke, for court papers revealed that the Occidental Petroleum Company, not Hammer, had paid its $95 million cost. Moreover, the company had bought a number of his paintings at high prices and made several donations to other organizations in his name.

Hammer died in December 1990 shortly after his museum's opening, leaving behind an oily mess. Stockholder suits were placed challenging his petroleum company's gifts, and a niece placed a suit against his estate charging that he had defrauded his wife of her half-interest in the collection. The new museum, despite its heavy cost overruns, is underfunded and still partly unfinished. Its inexperienced management announced plans to try to cover the budgetary shortfall by opening two bookstores in its lobby and by developing its potential as a "kind of singles' hangout for the 1990s."

The case raises questions, obviously, about why the County Museum continued to court Dr. Hammer so assiduously when it had serious doubts (as it has now admitted) about both his collection and his reliability. But for potential deal makers, the lesson is clear: deal making for its own sake—without genuine philanthropic purpose and scruples—can lead only to disaster and disgrace.

Part Seven

—⊰⊱—

*Perspectives on
the Passage of Time*

Chapter Seventeen

—◦◦◦◦◦—

The Pitfalls
of Perpetuity

A striking characteristic of the vast array of American foundations is that a large majority are created to last "in perpetuity".

One important factor that has produced this pattern is surely sentimentality. A great many foundations are created by older donors well aware of *memento mori*. The prospect of death and the hope of remembrance hang over the proceedings. The idea of a permanent memorial in the form of a foundation has powerful force in those circumstances.

Creating a lasting foundation also has romantic or heroic aspect evident in the kind of language in which the case for perpetuity was traditionally couched. The following example comes from the trust indenture of a fine old Pennsylvania foundation: "There is a certain fascinating grandeur that fires the imagination in the idea of a great benevolent foundation rolling down through the ages, distributing its beneficence in an unhappy world forever and forever and forever." The rhetoric may have become less grandiloquent in recent years, but the instinctive attraction of creating something that presumably will endure through eternity has not disappeared.

At a less spiritual level, the perpetuity idea also seems to connect somehow to property rights and vested interests. The last time it was seriously questioned was during the 1969 tax-reform debate in Congress. Reflecting an old American skepticism about the sequestering of private wealth in perpetual trusts, Representative Wright Patman and Senator Albert Gore, Sr., proposed that the life span of new foundations be limited to twenty-five years beyond the donor's death.

The howl of protest that immediately followed their proposal was revealing. Advocates for the wealthy charged that ignorant populism was at work to destroy a fundamental right of private property. Foundation professionals joined this opposition with a vehemence and unanimity that suggested a sensitive nerve of self-interest had been touched. That nerve was the chance that their employment might at some point be terminated if the provision were enacted. This possibility was very threatening in the philanthropic world, the idea of tenure having by then been widely absorbed into philanthropy from academia. Faced with such protests, Patman and Gore backed off. The proposal was dropped, and the idea of perpetuity has not been challenged in Congress since.

Looking at the matter against the broad background of world history, and indeed against that of American experience as well, it is extremely curious that the notion has somehow prevailed that foundations, like wine, improve with age. For although American foundations in general are less than a hundred years old (the great majority are less than half that age), the evidence is rather persuasive that time is not the friend of foundation vigor and effectiveness. In fact, with the passing of years decay and stagnation are quite common, if not epidemic.

The foregoing chapters have recounted a good many examples. Among the smaller family foundations, neglect or discord tends to grow with each successive generation, sometimes geometrically. There are admirable exceptions, but they are exceptions. Among the larger foundations, a frequent pattern is that after an initial fruitful period, a kind of creeping bureaucratization takes over, or an academic blight descends. They do not often erupt in conflict or corruption; they just fall quietly into obsolescence.

Perhaps because these difficulties have not generally been advertised, and indeed have most often been submerged under a great deal of self-congratulatory publicity issued by foundations themselves, donors and potential donors have not been made aware of some of the hazards of establishing foundations in perpetuity. Hence the sentimental and romantic impulses for perpetual remembrance have prevailed.

In fact, there is no clear and convincing basis for the contention that the quality of foundation performance increases with the passage of time. Indeed, among the more prominent foundations there is as much evidence of stagnation, fragmentation, and bureaucratization of programs over time as there is of steady improvement.

In broader historical perspective there may indeed be reason to believe that—over a longer period than the relatively brief century in which American foundations have proliferated—processes of decay and entropy may be inherent to their very nature.

The proclivity of American donors to opt for perpetuity in organizing their philanthropies also ignores the experience of other nations and cultures over many centuries in the past. The example of the great Roman Catholic charitable institutions may be pertinent in this regard.

Animated by powerful religious fervor and associated with a living church, the early monastic foundations flourished for several centuries. But by the eleventh century monks were spending much of their time in the chase, in taverns, and in brothels. Observers like the poet Chaucer called them "a walking libel on everything sacred." A century later things improved somewhat with the birth of the mendicant friars, the Dominicans and the Franciscans, but by the fourteenth century these too had degenerated. The mendicants had become a public nuisance, selling indulgences and fraudulent holy objects, living luxuriously, and quarreling endlessly among themselves. The result was a crack-down by the Council of Vienna on the corrupt practices of the administrators of church foundations. In the late-fifteenth century Pope Innocent VI, because of widespread stealing by the monks and the fact that two-thirds of them were living in concubinage, carried out another drastic program of reforms.

But a century later things were as bad as ever. Jurisdictional warfare among the religious orders and their foundations, involvement with politics, and general stagnation and corruption had reached the point that their original purposes—charitable work, care of the sick, teaching, meditation, and the advancement of learning—had been largely abandoned.

In addition, by the late Middle Ages the steady and ultimately gigantic accumulation of wealth in perpetual trusts by monastic orders came to be considered a threat to the economic development and stability of the various nations that harbored them. In that era they had accumulated ownership of up to half the land in England and France, for example. As a result, in one European country after another their privileged position was curbed, their holdings expropriated, and in some instances they were outlawed.

These developments throughout Europe led the great eighteenth-century French economist Turgot to conclude that the charitable perpetuity "bears within itself an irremediable defect which belongs to its very nature—the impossibility of maintaining its fulfillment. Founders deceive themselves vastly if they imagine that their zeal can be communicated from age to age to persons employed to perpetuate its effect. There is no body that in the long run has not lost the spirit of its first origin."

Historically, therefore, such encapsulated institutions have an impressive record of steady degeneration over any long span of years. It would be foolish to draw any direct parallels between the underlying causes of these historic calamities and the problems of modern foundations. But it would be equally foolish to dismiss some disquieting points of similarity. Today's foundations may in fact bear the same "irremediable defect" that Turgot identified and be vulnerable to the same loss of "the spirit of their first origin" for the same basic reasons.

In contemporary terms, foundations are institutions that are not subject to the effective discipline of external forces—whether voters, customers, stockholders, or even students—nor of a clear and objective measure of performance, such as a profit-and-loss statement. With their own secure and permanent source of income, they are encapsulated—thoroughly insulated—from the necessities and pressures that force most institutions to exert themselves to produce, adapt, and survive.

In the American system, governmental authority—executive,

legislative, and judicial—gives foundations very wide program latitude and does not attempt to exercise any review of or control over the quality or effectiveness of their work. In 1969 Congress imposed some much-needed rules to prevent tax-evading abuses by donors, and it has occasionally conducted highly partisan investigations of the ideological conformity of foundations, but on the whole, government has not interfered with their freedom of action.

This has been a boon to those few foundations inclined to tackle controversial problems or try risky new ventures. But it also permits a foundation inclined to doze to do so undisturbed almost indefinitely.

This is particularly a problem because the usual private sources from which outside review, stimulus, and criticism might come have been regrettably inoperative. The press and the academic community, for example, have generally been passive and silent, the press usually finding little of reader interest in foundations and not disposed to do investigative reporting on them. Academics, however much complaint they express privately, have remained publicly mute on the subject of foundations, perhaps immobilized by the fear that criticism would jeopardize their chances of obtaining grants.

Theoretically, foundation trustees could be a source of "independent" and "external" evaluation and criticism, but experience indicates that if they prod at all it tends to be with a feather-light touch. Like other governance mechanisms in American life, from corporate boards of directors to the U.S. Congress itself, foundation boards are frequently deficient in their performance—and typically, more deficient as the lifespan of a foundation stretches on.

Given these generally non-operative sources of external stimulus and oversight, and with their own secure and permanent sources of funds, endowed foundations can—and a good many do—come to rest undisturbed and unproductive in their little cocoons indefinitely.

In the face of the evidence of American experience, and of historical experience elsewhere, and perhaps of the inherent tendencies toward entropy and stagnation, if not corruption, of encapsulated entities like endowed foundations, why has the practice of endowing them in perpetuity not been effectively challenged? At least one great leader in philanthropy, Julius Rosenwald, has seriously tried.

An outstanding business entrepreneur as well as a philanthropist, Rosenwald was a strong and articulate believer in the stimulative effects of need and competition upon nonprofit institutions. He saw permanent endowments as an obstacle to the operation of these wholesome forces. In his view they tended to sap the energies not only of foundations, but of nonprofits in general.

"I am a great believer," Rosenwald once said, "that institutions which deserve support will find supporters and when the time comes that an institution is not needed it should not be hampered by endowment funds to prevent it from going out of existence."

Among American donors Rosenwald was the most articulate and determined early opponent of establishing foundations in perpetuity. Indeed, there are those who feel that his greatest contribution to philanthropy was his insistent and profound argumentation against the idea. In his various writings he put forth a number of strong arguments, some of them quite original. For example, he felt the notion itself was a hangover from ancient rituals and superstitious beliefs, a modern version of the ancient practice of burying a man's property with him after his death. He felt that the motivation of many donors in setting up perpetual trusts was to glorify their own name, a spurious and sterile kind of immortality in his view. He also argued that pledging funds for eternity "tends to lessen the amount available for immediate needs; and our immediate needs are too plain and too urgent" for that. He believed that a donor with clear objectives should focus his funds so as to maximize their impact, to make an all-out attack on problems, not a hedged and deferred one.

Implicit in the idea of withholding funds from present and known needs to provide for future and unknown ones was, in Rosenwald's view, an assumption that somehow future generations of Americans would not be willing or able to give generously to deal with the problems of their time. He, on the contrary, was confident "that those who follow us will be every bit as humane and enlightened, energetic and able, as we are, and the needs of the future can safely be left to be met by the generations of the future."

Consistent with these views, Rosenwald stipulated in setting up his own foundation that all of its funds had to be spent within twenty-five years of his death. He urged that all philanthropic enterprises "should come to an end with the close of the philanthropist's life, or at most, a single generation after his death." By his ardent preaching and his own example, he persuaded some of his contemporaries to shorten the term of their endowments. A limited number of recent donors, including Max Fleischmann, John Olin and Lucille Markey, and Mrs. Aaron Diamond, have followed his example.

But such a voice is now rarely heard, certainly among the professionals in philanthropy. That is a serious loss, for the question of the life span and duration of a donor's endowment deserves the most careful and thoughtful consideration.

Perpetuity is indeed a very long time.

Chapter Eighteen

—◦❧◦—

Trustees
and Trustworthiness
The Carnegie Case

Foundations are living organisms. They have money and power. They are organized, directed, and operated by human beings with all their virtues and faults. And over time the locus of control over foundation policies and the distribution of their funds can and does shift—despite the classical organizational theory that the donor sets the basic course, the trustees faithfully follow his or her intent in their policy decisions, and the chief executive follows the board's directives in overseeing operations.

That tidy, hierarchical, and static paradigm has of course little resemblance to the realities within actual foundations. Indeed, the departures from this theoretical pattern are so frequent and so great that it must be regarded as, if not quite a myth, then at least as a great simplification.

In actuality, the distribution of power and control within foundations shifts greatly and repeatedly with the passage of time. Donors can be quite clear—or very vague—about their intent in establishing a foundation; boards can be weak, strong, united or divided in setting policies after the donor has departed; and chief executives can be passive, confused, or commanding. For example, there have been major donors—such as Henry Ford, Howard Hughes, and John MacArthur—who left their trustees no real policy or program guidance other than legal boilerplate language. In such cases the donor makes himself virtually a nonfactor from the start. At the other extreme there have been donors like Buck Duke, who, in setting up his Duke Endowment, not only specified its general purposes but also the unalterable list of permitted grantees and the percentage of the foundation's income to be given to each. In between these extremes there have been many shadings, from broad and ambiguous guidance to narrow and precise restrictions.

Depending on circumstances, personalities, and even chance, the locus or distribution of controlling influence over the policies and programs of a foundation—especially a larger one—can shift greatly and repeatedly over the years. The forces at work are so subtle and complex, and generally so hidden, that no general patterns can be demonstrated. But, to illustrate how the dynamics of these power flows can operate, examination of an actual and important "best case" may be instructive, namely that of Andrew Carnegie and his Carnegie Corporation, as his central philanthropy was confusingly called.

Andrew Carnegie was, of course, one of the greatest American donors ever. His belief in and his interest in philanthropy was almost unparalleled. He had a fully developed philosophy of the charitable responsibilities of the rich, articulated in his famous "Gospel of Wealth" and other writings. Throughout his life he gave generously, and by the end he had committed virtually all of his great fortune to philanthropy.

He was an exceptionally entrepreneurial and experienced donor, having created a series of outstanding philanthropic institutions during his lifetime, from the Carnegie Institute and the libraries project to his Foundation for the Advancement of Teaching and his Endowment for International Peace. His personally written statements of policies and objectives for these creations were models of thoughtfulness, clarity, and practicality.

Carnegie was a man of extraordinary breadth of interests in education, science, culture, and international affairs. He also had a remarkably wide acquaintance with outstanding leaders in many fields of American life—from government officials and business people to intellectuals, scholars, and scientists. In the formation of his various philanthropies he brought his own extensive experience in creating and developing new organizations to bear, as well as his wide range of acquaintance in nonprofit fields. The boards of trustees he assembled were not mere sets of old business cronies but rather groups of distinguished and strong individuals.

Carnegie's own wealth and prestige enabled him to attract such leaders to his philanthropies, and he gave them his full trust in carrying out their responsibilities. His statement of confidence in the fidelity and capability of foundation trustees is perhaps the classic on the subject. In 1911, when setting up his final and most comprehensive philanthropy, the Carnegie Corporation, he wrote: "As in all human institutions, there will be fruitful seasons and slack seasons. But as long as it exists there will come, from time to time, men into its control and management who will have vision and energy and wisdom, and the perpetual foundation will have a new birth of usefulness and service."

Thus this man, with his almost unparalleled competence and experience as a donor, should have done as well as a donor could possibly hope to do in setting up a new major foundation. Clearly, his hopes remained high, for he bequeathed the huge remainder of his estate to this philanthropic "Corporation" at the end of his life.

How, in fact, did his hopes and plans turn out after his death in 1919? The story, spanning more than seventy years, breaks into four chapters—the Betrayal, the Slump, the Muddle, and the Renaissance—and the final chapters are yet to be written.

The Betrayal

Carnegie named to the board of his Corporation the heads of the five principal philanthropic institutions he had previously created, plus his financial and personal secretaries. Even though it was pointed out to him that the situation of the institutional trustees was inherently conflicted, since they would be both distributors and beneficiaries of the funds, he ignored that advice. (It was not until 1946 that these ex officio trustees were finally dropped from the board.) He also reserved to himself the right to administer the foundation as long as he lived, which he did from 1911 until 1919. During that period, the board met only once a year merely to ratify decisions he had already made. So despite his protestations of confidence in his trustees, as long as he was alive he behaved dictatorially.

Almost as soon as he was dead, these confusions and contradictions produced serious problems. Carnegie had left a foundation with almost no qualified staff and with a board dominated by built-in grantees. Within three years they had appropriated nearly

$40 million without benefit of long-range planning or serious consideration of the impact of the spending spree on the foundation's future. Because the charter required that grant commitments could be paid only from the foundation's income (then some $6 million a year) and not from capital, programs for the next fifteen years were severely restricted. Not surprisingly, the bulk of this money went to institutions represented on the foundation's board.

Was this a betrayal by the board? Did Carnegie provoke it by his own conduct and his questionable choices of eminent but conflicted trustees? Certainly it was a grab of money for their own institutions. But since those institutions were creations of Carnegie himself, it could not be called an improper diversion of funds to unauthorized purposes. Still, though not unlawful, it seems at least a bit greedy.

Soon thereafter the substance, spirit, and general thrust of the Corporation's programs were radically redirected. Fortunately, the archives of Carnegie's papers and those of the Corporation are now accessible to scholars so some old secrets are being revealed. The following account draws on the most substantial and widely praised of these studies to date, Ellen Lagemann's *The Politics of Knowledge: The Carnegie Corporation, Philanthropy, and Public Policy* (Hanover, N.H.: University Press of New England, 1989).

The Carnegie Corporation's two most influential and ambitious trustees in the 1920s were Henry Pritchett, head of the Carnegie Foundation for the Advancement of Teaching and former president of the Massachusetts Institute of Technology, and Elihu Root, a prominent attorney, Nobel Laureate, and former U. S. secretary of war and secretary of state. They envisaged the foundation not as a mere dispenser of benefactions but as a private instrument to foster "reforms." Their general approach was to use the foundation to create powerful nongovernmental agencies of scientists and experts to counter what they regarded as dangerous populistic influences threatening traditional American values and the power of the established Anglo-Saxon elite.

In carrying out their grand new design for the foundation, Pritchett and Root led it to make a series of substantial grants to the National Research Council "to organize science," to a new National Bureau of Economic Research, and to the American Law Institute. Their ostensible purpose was to introduce more "scientific management" into the nation's affairs. But their urgent concern in taking these actions was what they regarded as the growing threat of immigrants, blacks, demagogues, laborites, socialists, and others of "inferior heredity, morals, and understanding of business and American-style democracy."

The purpose in supporting the National Research Council was partly to counter the "pacifistic" tendencies of some scientists, which Pritchett and Root felt were inhibiting the development of new military technology. The National Bureau of Economic Research grew out of a backdrop of mounting industrial tension and violence and the hope of prominent businessmen that these dangers could be prevented by gathering the recommendations of a private group of "experts."

In the field of economics, Pritchett's interest was explicitly in economic "propaganda" to counter the appeal of "popular agitators." To this end, he at one point even recommended that the Carnegie Corporation purchase an independent newspaper, the *Washington Post*. (In the end the idea was dropped not on grounds of impropriety but because Root and others thought it would be "a bad investment.")

In 1923 another initiative was taken to create the American Law Institute (ALI) in response to a fear that the "intrusion" of immigrants and the lower classes into the legal profession constituted a national danger. Trustee Root, in a speech to the New York State Bar Association a few years earlier, had deplored the fact that "50 percent of the lawyers in this city are either foreign born or arc of foreign-born parents and the great mass of them . . . have in the blood necessarily the traditions of the countries from which they came."

In the words of Ellen Lagemann, ALI was "a means of dealing with pressing social problems in ways that would advance the interest and priorities of elites within the legal profession." It would not be too severe to say that in its support for ALI and its other large initiatives in its first years, the underlying agenda of the Corporation was not only elitist but racist—not only to help preserve the dominant position of a particular segment of American society but also to preserve its "racial purity." The trustees were explicitly worried about "the alien stream flowing into our citizenship," and they made the foundation a leading supporter of eugenics studies at the time, some of which urged policies of selective breeding and forced sterilization of the "unfit."

During this period the original Carnegie trustees provided a repugnant example of self-interest, class bias, and usurpation of power by members of a nonfamily board. Providing grants to set up private agencies to influence public policy—forerunners of what are now called think tanks—they not only clearly understood the potential power of private funds to shape public opinion and government policy, but they also were determined to utilize and exploit that power for their own purposes.

In so doing they were in a sense following the kind of thing Carnegie had done in setting up his Endowment for International Peace, but there was a difference: Carnegie's initiatives had been in behalf of such goals as creating opportunities for the average citizen to have access to books for self-development and for the general advancement of science, education and world peace. He came from a poor family, he was himself an immigrant, and he had lifted himself by his own bootstraps. He was a descendant of old Scottish radicals, he had battled against unfair and unequal privilege, and he believed in the unlimited potential of the common man.

This is not to say that Carnegie was saintly and benign in all his business dealings, or clear and consistent in marking out the purposes of his philanthropies. Indeed, like the other industrialists of his time, he was a tough opponent of the trade unions, and in his philanthropy he could be erratic and impulsive—giving pipe organs to churches even though he was not religious, and offering medals for personal acts of heroism. Nevertheless, the spirit of his philanthropy was always democratic, hopeful, and constructive. That within five years of his death his Corporation turned into a racist and reactionary operation to defend the privileges of the old WASP elite and block the advancement of immigrants and the underprivileged was an ugly deformation of his spirit and intent. And ironically it was perpetrated by a group of gentlemen of high reputation and the utmost respectability.

What does this say about Carnegie's absolute trust in trustees? Was it perhaps some fault, some pretentiousness, in the man himself that caused him to entrust his great philanthropic creations to a group of individuals whose background and social class biases were fundamentally contradictory to his own?

The Slump

The outburst of activist and politicized philanthropy in the Carnegie Corporation lasted until 1923, when Francis Keppel, a personable young man and a certified member of the WASP establishment, was hired as president. He headed the Carnegie Corporation for the next nineteen years. If the underlying agenda and the ulterior purposes of the preceding regime had been grandiose and sinister, those of Keppel's long tenure were random, inconsequential, and even silly.

Simultaneously with Keppel's appointment, seven new trustees were added and the balance of forces on the board changed significantly. The Corporation dropped its crusade to save the nation from newcomers and shifted to a program to uplift the cultural level of the general citizenry. Why this new direction was chosen is still difficult to understand. Perhaps it was done in a spirit of resignation: If the great unwashed were irreversibly going to be with us, then the foundation might at least try to wash them. Whatever the reasoning, the projects actually funded were rather peculiar, even quaint.

The general idea was to attract the multitudes into adult education centers, the art museums, and—in at least one tie to Andrew Carnegie—the libraries. Exposing the ordinary citizenry to classical art and literature, it was believed (and stated), would improve their character, judgment, and tastes—and in addition would promote social stability. In the end, and by virtually every measure, the effort failed miserably.

Keppel was a warm and likeable person, but he was an ineffective executive, and for the head of a major foundation, his social outlook was remarkably narrow. The 1920s and 1930s, when he was in charge, were years marked by severe strain and friction in American life, exacerbated by growing international dangers. By the early 1930s a devastating depression had struck, followed by the period of the New Deal, and when Keppel retired, World War II was already raging in Europe. Yet his gracefully written annual reports contain hardly a hint of the great issues and problems of the times. In the isolated environment of the Corporation, training for librarians, adult education conferences, and the distribution of art teaching sets continued to be the preoccupation. Keppel's tenure was a time of endlessly trivial pursuits.

During Keppel's final years as president the foundation commissioned what it intended to be a study of how the "uplift" of blacks could be addressed through cultural projects. By mistake they chose a Swedish economist, Gunnar Myrdal, to head it. The result was a classic and highly controversial report on the general problem of race relations in America, a report that powerfully influenced later progress toward racial integration. However, the foundation was so embarrassed and dismayed by the outcome that it did everything but disavow the study after it was published.

How, in a second period of basic shift in the foundation's direction following the donor's death, did his keystone foundation come to focus on matters that he would probably have regarded as peripheral, if not preposterous? Why had trustees appointed by Carnegie so quickly abandoned his aims and violated his values? Why, later, did they fail utterly to bring to the foundation's programs and priorities some awareness of the sweeping changes taking place in American society and in the world? And how did it happen that a hired president of extremely modest capability was left undisturbed by the trustees to head the institution for some twenty years? In that long period how could they not bring themselves to replace him?

The Muddle

After the two initial phases in the foundation's post-Carnegie history—the Betrayal and the Slump (which scholars have now euphemistically designated as its periods of "scientific philanthropy" and "cultural philanthropy")—came thirteen years of muddle (1942–55). During this crucial period of wartime and postwar developments the foundation fell under the leadership of three ineffective presidents in a row.

Is such a span of years a reasonable turnaround time for an organization with perfect freedom to change its direction and with only a handful of staff? What about board responsibility to face a foundation's problems and address its own mistakes?

The Renaissance

Some thirty-five years after Carnegie's death, his foundation finally entered a fruitful period of vigorous programs reasonably related to the spirit and concerns of the donor and relevant to the needs of the times. It happened not by virtue of planning and policy setting by the board, but almost by a fortunate accident.

In 1946 John Gardner, a young psychologist who had served as an officer in the U.S. Marines in World War II, was hired as a program officer. By that time the board was an ossified body, and the staff was virtually leaderless. Gardner quickly showed his abilities in the design of several promising new programs in the field of research on foreign regions of the world. He thereby became the obvious choice to succeed the foundation's ill and incapacitated president, John Dollard, which he did in 1955.

Almost immediately thereafter, the foundation moved forward in a program of "strategic philanthropy" to study and recommend changes in public policies on major national questions, especially education. Gardner proved to be a master strategist and practitioner in the technique of using foundation funds and ideas to affect the policies and programs of other institutions, especially government. In this first initiative he made the goal of "excellence and equality" in American education his mission. With the help of his able vice president, James Perkins, he then pursued that goal on several fronts simultaneously.

First, several important educational research projects and experiments were financed. Next, prestigious commissions of both laymen and experts were formed to study the nation's educational problems and to recommend solutions. The publication of their reports was carefully timed to produce maximum impact on policy makers. In parallel, Gardner, through his own cogent and elegant essays and books, played an important public advocacy role.

Within the foundation Gardner's sheer ability and force of personality enabled him in effect to take control of its policies and programs. By 1964 his influence had begun to reach far beyond the corporation, and he had become a national figure and force. In that year President Lyndon Johnson asked him to head a major task force on education. The resulting report led to the Elementary and Secondary Education Act passed by Congress in 1965—landmark legislation that established clearly and finally the responsibility of the federal government in this crucial field.

To no one's great surprise, Gardner was called to Washington the following year to become secretary of the Department of Health, Education, and Welfare. By then the Carnegie Corporation had finally regained the level of prestige that its founder had enjoyed as a philanthropist a half-century earlier. Gardner's position was filled by another very able man, Alan Pifer, who had served under him and who quickly assumed firm control. Pifer's ardent cause was that of social and economic justice, and he preached eloquently and incessantly for the federal government to accept its responsibility to help achieve those goals. Shortly after he took over, the foundation enjoyed a quick triumph by its sponsorship of the Commission on Public Television, which reported its findings in early 1967. Within a month President Johnson recommended passage of the Public Broadcasting Act. Congress did so in November of that same year, bringing into being the Public Broadcasting System. Actually, Gardner (from his new post in HEW) had been an important moving force in the event, but PBS brought much acclaim to the Carnegie Corporation and gave Pifer a running start.

Pifer's second major initiative was also a carryover from the Gardner period, namely, the creation of the Carnegie Commission on Higher Education to make a comprehensive study of the future financing problems of colleges and universities, which were then beginning to drown under a huge influx of new students funded by the so-called GI Bill giving educational grants to World War II veterans. Clark Kerr, former chancellor of the University of California, was named to head the work. Ultimately the group, with $12 million of foundation funds, published scores of reports and monographs on every aspect of the problems of the nation's complex and growing system of higher education. These significantly influenced the policies of both the government and the schools themselves thereafter.

Another achievement under Pifer was the creation of the popular educational program *Sesame Street* and the Children's Television Workshop, which has become an influential national and international institution.

As the years progressed, and as the nation became more troubled socially and more conservative politically, Pifer was an increasingly ardent proponent of liberal policy positions. In a sense he became as radical in his support of the rights of the poor and disadvantaged as old Andrew Carnegie had been in his attacks on the English Establishment and its treatment of the Scots in the nineteenth century. Consistently, the grants of the foundation under Pifer's leadership were focused on support for the more promising and influential new advocates for the disadvantaged.

Unlike Gardner, who simply accepted the rather passive Establishment board he had inherited, Pifer from the beginning of his term took a strong hand in the selection of more liberal and more diverse trustees as resignations and retirements occurred.

By the late 1960s the board had been converted from a virtually all-white, all-male Establishment body to a more diverse group including women, blacks, Hispanics, and Jews. This became an important protection for Pifer as his militantly stated views became increasingly out of step with the nation's mood under Presidents Nixon and Reagan.

The Gardner and Pifer periods raise interesting questions. Both were vigorous, effective leaders who took the foundation in directions that were finally in the spirit and style of old Andrew Carnegie. Their accomplishments would surely have given him much pride and satisfaction.

But was Gardner's presidency—given his elegance of style as well as the brilliance of his ideas—simply another example of trustees riding along passively on a purposeful president's train, as they had ridden for years on one that was going nowhere, namely Keppel's? And did Pifer, by carefully reshaping the board in a liberal direction in accordance with his views, not violate at least the theoretical concept of presidential subservience to the policy authority residing with the board? Whatever the answers to those questions, the Gardner–Pifer period in the history of the Carnegie Corporation was indubitably a time of renaissance after several uninspiring decades.

In 1982 Pifer retired and was succeeded by Dr. David Hamburg, who in a lower key has pursued policies generally in line with those laid down by Pifer. Hamburg has increasingly focused the efforts of the foundation on the problems of early childhood development. Drawing on the advice of the most-respected authorities in the field, he has made Carnegie a less controversial but no less influential factor on the national scene. He also has taken an active hand in reshaping the board to his interests and style.

So what are some of the lessons, the morals, of the Carnegie story in understanding the processes of control, change, and development in foundations, particularly the larger ones, over the long term?

That change and diversion of a foundation's purposes over time are inevitable, and that donors should realistically understand and accept that fact?

Or that a donor should try to tie down the objectives of his foundation so tightly and specifically that they cannot be abandoned or subverted, ever?

Or that if the foundation of a donor as wise and experienced as Carnegie can encounter such grave problems for decades at a stretch, then the prospects are even worse for donors who are more ordinary mortals?

Or that time has proven the wisdom of Andrew Carnegie's faith that over the long term, and despite periods of decline, "the perpetual foundation will have a new birth of usefulness and service"?

Perhaps all of the above, plus the insight that as a realist and idealist, Carnegie took out ample insurance against diversion of his ultimate general-purpose foundation by his strategy of spreading his philanthropic bets—that is, by creating in addition a number of separate special-purpose philanthropic institutions.

After three-quarters of a century, all of these institutions have remained productive and on course:

The Endowment for International Peace has had its ups and downs and its intervals of controversy, but it has evolved with the times and is now a significant factor in professional and public discussions of foreign policy issues.

The old Carnegie Institute in Pittsburgh has now merged into a major, high-quality university, Carnegie–Mellon.

The Carnegie Institution of Washington has now been overtaken in scale and importance by a number of new government-sponsored research institutions, but it continues to be a useful and well-regarded scientific center.

The Carnegie Foundation for the Advancement of Teaching—in addition to its early triumph as sponsor of the Flexner report that helped reform American medical education—has spawned two significant offspring: the massively successful and influential Teachers' Insurance and Annuity Association and the Educational Testing Service, both self-supporting and of national significance. The CFAT itself has also been a useful vehicle for conducting educational surveys and policy studies financed by the Carnegie Corporation.

This amounts to a very good batting average by the old Scot.

—☙❧—

Conclusion

Philanthropy and the Future

For more than two hundred years the United States has been building a formidable tradition of charitable giving, foundation formation, and citizen volunteering. Most of our principal philanthropists in that history remain relatively unknown, at least as compared with our political, military, and industrial figures. Still, the saga has had its heroes, its failures and its mediocrities. It has also had its huge and almost overlooked but most heroic factor of all, namely, the kindly, giving, volunteering spirit and habits of the American people by the millions.

Looking back, the nation can revel in the unparalleled number of its foundations and in their splendid achievements, even as it must—at times—cringe over their occasional calamitous failures. It can take pride in the success of some great philanthropic inventions, such as the now rapidly proliferating community foundations, just as it can worry about the creeping spread of ethical problems from the spheres of business and politics into some institutions of the nonprofit sector.

So the saga of American philanthropy is an ongoing, unfolding story, and a major new chapter of that story is about to open. The United States at this moment is full of problems; it is also full of millionaires. This is a happy coincidence, for the nation's unique tradition of private philanthropy may now offer one of its most useful instruments for finding solutions to those problems.

That prospect is threatened, however, by some deep underlying trends in American society that impact philanthropy in crucial ways. Of particular concern are the giving patterns of the nation's wealthiest individuals, since they are the fountainhead from which major benefactions flow. They are also the source of new private grant-making foundations—the uniquely powerful and creative American instrumentality for social, scientific, and educational advancement.

But that fountainhead may dribble rather than gush unless some changes in attitudes can be made to occur—attitudes that are based on deep human habits and instincts about property, family, and narrow self-interest. That is the dark shadow that falls over a potentially very bright prospect.

It is cast by two brutal facts that have become increasingly evident over the past few years: First, the income and the accumulated wealth of Americans at the most affluent levels have increased very much faster than that of the average American; and second, wealthy Americans are very much less charitable in proportion to their wealth and income than are average and poorer Americans.

According to the estimates of leading statisticians, the United

obligation to give something back to the society and to sustain its tradition of social responsibility.

So much for the evidence of indifference among many very wealthy Americans to any philanthropic obligations during their active working lives.

But are the scales brought into better balance, and are the wealthy more disposed to commit some of their accumulated wealth to philanthropy as they plan their "estates" toward the end of their lives? Is it at this point that a corrective burst of generosity and social concern tends to occur? If it should, the consequences could be immense, for the present magnitude of that accumulated private wealth is staggering.

Periodic estimates of private wealth are made available from official data: In 1976, for example, there were an estimated 180,000 American millionaires; in 1982, 470,000; and in 1986, 941,000, more than a fivefold increase in little more than a decade.

In the U.S. Treasury's *Statistics of Income Bulletin* for spring 1993, a still-higher estimate was published by two respected statisticians, Barry Johnson and Marvin Schwartz. By their calculations, the net worth of the top American wealth-holders, representing less than 2 percent of the adult population, totaled more than $4.8 trillion and accounted for between 25 and 30 percent of the total personal wealth in the United States. This reflected an eighteen-fold increase in the number of American millionaires in the decade between 1976–1986.

Examining the estate-tax returns of decedents with assets of $500,000 or more for the year 1986 (who numbered 8,990), these scholars found that their charitable bequests amounted to 24 percent of the total assets, for a grand total of $41.6 billion. In death these wealthy individuals were substantially more generous than in life—an encouraging finding.

In 1993 Robert Avery of Cornell University, an economist specializing in the study of wealth, published a new set of findings on the prospective intergenerational transfers of wealth in the United States that have stirred both great hopes and great controversy. (For a number of years before moving to the university Avery directed the wealth surveys of the Federal Reserve Board, and he is recognized as a leading authority.) Using data from the 1989 U.S. government Survey of Consumer Finances, Avery forecasted bequests totaling $10.4 trillion (adjusted for inflation) between 1990 and 2040. With appropriate cautions, he has predicted an average of about $225 billion a year in total bequests as today's wealth-holders die off. What proportion of these immense anticipated transfers will go for charitable purposes? The averages of the past suggest that something near 1 percent of the total will be so allocated.

If these estimates prove to be even approximately correct, the benefits to the nonprofit sector will be close to colossal—on the order of some $2 billion a year. These new resources for the sector would be in addition to the annual contributions of living donors and contributors. They are of a scale almost to transform it.

Obviously such projections contain fairly wide margins of error. But they represent the best estimates that present economic and statistical techniques can offer. And they are encouraging. Coming at a time of great national distress, governmental gridlock, and severe strain on available resources to address social, educational, and health needs, such a volume of new resources for the nonprofit sector could be more than a boon; they could be an instrument of national rescue.

Recent decades have been a period of great economic growth in the United States and of intensive wealth accumulation. Without descending to describe the period as one of "greed," there is no doubt that it has been a slack season for the launching of major new philanthropies, and a time of general shortage of brilliant, creative donorship.

The base of the great American tradition of generosity and civic engagement, however, remains solid and strong. The annual totals of charitable contributions and volunteering in the country are a regular reminder of the vitality of that ethic. But it is to be hoped that once again and before long, as has happened in the past, a truly great new donor advocate and standard setter—on the order of Andrew Carnegie, John D. Rockefeller, or Julius Rosenwald—will appear to reinvigorate a noble national tradition.

It is quite possible that that figure is already among us—namely, George Soros. He has a great and intense philanthropic vision: the reestablishment of open societies in the former Communist totalitarian world, including both the Soviet Union and its former satellites, as well as mainland China.

By his initiatives Soros is not only preaching a Gospel of Wealth as Andrew Carnegie did in his time; he is demonstrating the capacity of a passionate and creative philanthropist actually to alter the course of history in behalf of human freedom.

Nor will Soros have to belabor the point that the "man who dies rich dies disgraced." The impact of his example in itself might be sufficient to persuade the new generation of wealthy Americans to dedicate a fraction—perhaps a fifth—of their fortunes to the well-being of humanity. They can then count on the vast, strong charitable tradition among non-rich Americans to accomplish the rest. Together they can help build a better world.

—⚜—

Epilogue
Dos and Don'ts for Donors

You are wealthy. You are successful. It is time for some new personal growth. Also, maybe it is time to start paying back something to the society that made it all possible. Philanthropy may be your best vehicle for accomplishing all that.

If you take that path here are some dos and don'ts that may be helpful:

1. Get started early. Deathbed philanthropy is deadly. But philanthropy as part of your active life can be a great new and satisfying adventure. So start soon on your apprenticeship. Learn the work. Discover the problems and the possibilities. Make it an ongoing part of your life.

2. Give yourself as well as your money. Involve yourself, your ideas, your energy, your leadership. This is a field for entrepre-

neurship, for creativity as well as dutifulness. Your abilities will increase the value of any money you give by large multiples. And giving of yourself will greatly increase your own satisfactions.

3. Choose the instrument or vehicle of your philanthropy carefully. You have a number of options. You can give directly to an established institution—a hospital, church, or university. You can give a fund of any size, small or large, to a community foundation. You can set up an operating foundation or a grant-making foundation. Each has its advantages and limitations. Learn them, weigh them, and choose the one that fits you. Or choose more than one. But choose knowledgeably, and understand realistically the capabilities and the deficiencies of each for your purposes.

4. If you involve the family in your plans (a very common and natural impulse), do not do so on the assumption that a family foundation is a reliable means of "keeping the family together." On the contrary, over time most such foundations breed clashes and competitiveness. So do not try to bind the members into forced collaboration forever. Give them the option of splitting the foundation up at some point; or create it for a limited number of years— thirty or forty, perhaps. Or set it up as a "donor-advised fund" within a community foundation. Above all, do not try to rule or manipulate your family from the grave via your foundation. That can lead only to disaster and to the befouling of your own memory.

5. If your aim is to create a permanent memorial for yourself or your family, a foundation is a risky option. Better to build that memorial into the body of an established, deeply rooted institution such as a church, hospital, museum, library, or research center. An endowed chapel, laboratory, scholarship fund, dormitory, special book collection, arboretum, or concert series is far more likely to be an ongoing, useful asset in your community (and a re-

spected memorial to you or your family a hundred years after your death) than any freestanding foundation you might create.

6. Selecting the trustees for your foundation is another area in which you must make an effort to be realistic rather than impulsive or sentimental. Take the matter very seriously. It is easy just to name some family members, your lawyer, and a couple of old business colleagues and call that a board of trustees. But do you want a board that will simply be congenial and deferential? The alternative, a strong, independent board, may give you argument from time to time but be knowledgeable about the social problems you want to address. If the latter, have you defined the program objectives of the foundation clearly enough that you know the kinds of skills and experience that should be represented around the table?

The quality of the trustees you choose will have enormous impact on the effectiveness of your foundation and on its fidelity to your intentions after you are gone.

7. If your wealth is of moderate scale, or if your interest in philanthropy is less than consuming, or if you are not too knowledgeable about philanthropic giving, or if your family is fractious and full of stresses—yet you are interested in helping your home city or locality—consider seriously the option of placing your funds in a community foundation. It offers many philanthropic values and protections.

8. Remember that many of the business skills you have learned can apply in philanthropy as well: dealmaking, leveraging, entrepreneurship. Study the great masters, such as Andrew Carnegie, Mary Lasker, Jim Rouse, and George Soros, to multiply the impact of your gifts.

9. Take Julius Rosenwald's advice about the perils of perpetuity

very seriously. His words are among the wisest ever written for someone who has had the kind of successful career you have had.

10. There are certain dangerous pitfalls you should avoid. One is all the happy, self-congratulatory talk in the world of philanthropy about how almost without exception every project and program succeeds. Such foolishness readily flourishes in the absence of a bottom line for measuring results. It is obvious that American society, for all its successes, is now confronted with some deep and difficult problems. So make your best and bravest effort to solve them. There will be mistakes and failures; do not bury or deny them, nor be discouraged by them, but learn from them. Nothing this difficult and this important could possibly be easy.

11. Finally, remember that if you can be even nearly as successful in your philanthropy as you have been in your business or profession, you will have done great things for your family, your community, and your country, and you will have gained as much public respect and immortality as it is possible for a human being to achieve.

You will have taken full advantage of the opportunities for service offered by a particularly prosperous period in American history, and you will have made your full contribution as a citizen and benefactor to the future of a great democracy. So give your philanthropy not only your money, give it your best.

Index

Index

Index